# THE MYTH OF MEANING

# THE MYTH OF MEANING

## IN THE

# WORK OF C. G. JUNG

ANIELA JAFFÉ

translated by
R. F. C. HULL

I have seen many people die because life for them was
not worth living. From this I conclude that the question
of life's meaning is the most urgent question of all.

Camus

**DAIMON**
ZÜRICH

This edition is an adaptation of the 1970 printing by Hodder and Stoughton, London. It was translated from *Der Mythus vom Sinn* (1967), which is also available in a new edition in Daimon Verlag, Zürich (© 1983).

Front cover image: graphical adaptation of a Thracian labyrinth relief

Cover design and graphics: Joel T. Miskin

ISBN: 3 8560 500 4

Copyright © 1984,
Daimon Verlag, Postfach, CH-8032 Zürich, Switzerland

# CONTENTS

|  |  | *page* |
|---|---|---|
| | Foreword | 7 |
| 1 | The Theme | 11 |
| 2 | The Unconscious and the Archetype | |
| | *Hypothesis and Model* | 14 |
| | *The Archetype as Instinct and an Element of the Spirit* | 19 |
| | *The Psychoid Archetype* | 22 |
| | *Conscious Realisation as Discrimination* | 24 |
| 3 | Jung's Method and Style | 26 |
| 4 | The Hidden Reality | |
| | *Ordering Factors in Nature* | 29 |
| | *Science and Religion* | 34 |
| | *The Numinosity of the Unconscious* | 37 |
| | *Appearance and Reality* | 40 |
| | *The Numinosity of the Self* | 42 |
| | *A Kabbalistic Parallel* | 44 |
| | *A Theological Parallel (Paul Tillich)* | 47 |
| 5 | Inner Experience | |
| | *Alchemy as an Expression of Inner Experience* | 50 |
| | *The Unconscious as Inner Experience* | 52 |
| | *Modern Art as an Expression of Inner Experience* | 61 |
| | *Inner Experience through Mescalin and LSD* | 68 |
| 6 | Individuation | |
| | *Active Imagination and Life* | 76 |
| | *Historical Order and Eternal Order* | 85 |
| | *Freedom and Bondage* | 88 |
| 7 | Good and Evil | |
| | *The Human Conflict* | 95 |
| | *Will and Counter-Will in the God-Image* | 98 |
| 8 | Answer to Job | |
| | *Verbal Image and Object* | 101 |
| | *The Antinomy of the Holy (Paul Tillich)* | 104 |
| | *Jung's Subjective Testament* | 105 |
| | *The World's Suffering* | 108 |

# 6     CONTENTS

*page*

9   The Individuation of Mankind
     *The God-Image of the Holy Ghost*      112
     *Reconciling the Opposites in the God-Image*      119

10   Man in the Work of Redemption      122

11   The One Reality      128

12   The Individual      134

13   Meaning as the Myth of Consciousness
     *Creative Consciousness*      138
     *The Secret of Simplicity*      148
     *Synchronicity*      150

     Notes      155

     Bibliography      177

# FOREWORD

It was a radiant August day in 1940. In spite of the adversity
of the times, a small group of people had gathered together in
Moscia, at the Swiss end of Lago Maggiore, for a "symbolic"
Eranos meeting. That morning the Basel mathematician
Andreas Speiser had lectured on "The Platonic Doctrine of
the Unknown God and the Christian Trinity". It was the only
lecture that had been announced and we were supposed to be
satisfied with that this year. But things turned out differently.
In the afternoon C. G. Jung, who was one of the guests, withdrew to a shady corner of the garden by the shore of the lake.
He had fetched a Bible from the library, and sat there reading
it and making notes. Next day he surprised the tensely listening
audience with a reply to the disquisition of his Basel colleague.
Speaking extempore, he supplemented the theme with a lecture
on "The Psychology of the Trinity Idea".[1] In the way that was
characteristic of him, pondering his words and at times hesi-
tantly, he formulated thoughts he had been carrying around
with him for years but had not yet put into their final shape.

The stenogram of Jung's improvisation proved later to be
practically ready for press; only extensive insertions were
added. To anyone who knew Jung's method of working there
was nothing astonishing about this. He began writing only
when the thoughts were mature in him and he had collected
and verified the explanatory material. Often there was an
interval of many years between the first creative intuition and
its setting down in words; but from the moment he took up
his pen he was wholly under the spell of the nascent work. He
completed it in a single draft, working on it at set times daily,

often even during bouts of illness. Slow and deliberate as his
speech, the clear handwriting flowed across the paper. At a
subsequent re-reading, it was only technical additions, "ampli-
fications" drawn from every conceivable field of knowledge,
that were pasted in the wide margins of the folio sheets on
numerous small slips, some of them quite tiny. But the written
text as such remained for the most part untouched.

Jung's improvisation on the psychology of the Trinity idea
concluded the meeting in Moscia. It was followed by a serious
yet lively discussion on the terrace of Casa Eranos, with its
wide view of the lake and the mountains beyond. Jung was
relaxed and—a rare thing, especially in those years of catastrophe
—satisfied with his performance. Almost apologetically, though,
he distinguished his style from that of the previous speaker.
"I can formulate my thoughts only as they break out of me.
It is like a geyser. Those who come after me will have to put
them in order." This remark has to be taken with a grain of
salt, for it gives no inkling of the thoroughness, the positively
pedantic care with which the empirical material was assembled,
sifted, and intellectually worked over until the final form could
no longer be postponed. Even so, it does explain some of the
difficulties a reading of his works presents, especially those
written in old age. The very profusion of creative ideas and of
the material discussed opens out endless vistas, and the spon-
taneity of his style leads to occasional obscurities.

It was the memory of that summer talk by Lago Maggiore
that has given me the courage to single out for study one
particular thematic complex in Jung's work: how the interplay
of consciousness and the unconscious yielded for him an
answer to the perennial question: What is the meaning of life
and of man?

My especial thanks are due to Mrs Marianne Niehus-Jung,
who up to the time of her death in 1965 followed the progress

of the work with interest and permitted me to quote from the forthcoming volumes of Jung's letters.[2] Dr Gerhard Adler, their editor, likewise gave his consent. A number of friends aided me by word and deed during the preparation of the manuscript. I thank them all for their co-operation and patience. Also I would like to thank Mr R. F. C. Hull for many valuable suggestions during our collaboration on the English edition.

Zurich, autumn 1966.                    ANIELA JAFFÉ.

## FOREWORD TO THE SECOND EDITION

More than a decade has passed since the initial appearance of THE MYTH OF MEANING and today, more than ever, we are aware of the great relevance of the topics addressed by C. G. Jung. Once again it is clear that he was ahead of his time.

Jung's answer to the question of meaning is best understood in light of the abundance of problems which so deeply concerned him; for example, the phenomena of inner experience, of a transcendence of life and consciousness, and of the borders of perception. In his view, the relationship between psychology and the natural sciences is of crucial importance, as is that between psychology and religion.

The idea of the gradual expansion of human consciousness down through the centuries — 'the myth of meaning' — is central to his work. It culminates in a perception of the unity of being, whereby spirit and matter, science and faith, consciousness and unconsciousness are not considered to be opposites, but rather different aspects of one and the same reality.

Recent substantiation of this comes in certain observations made by the physicist Fritjof Capra and reported in his book, «The Turning Point». He discusses the many parallels between Jungian Psychology and modern science and remarks that: «Jung . . . used concepts that are surprisingly similar to the ones contemporary physicists use in their descriptions of subatomic phenomena.»[1] Analogous to the developments in modern science, Jung's path of perception leads beyond the one-sided, rational, mechanistic view of the world.

This book was conceived as a brief and easily understandable introduction to C. G. Jung's world of thought, with its great richness of themes. I would like to thank the Daimon Verlag for making this new edition available.

Zürich, March 1984                                  *Aniela Jaffé*

[1] Capra, Fritjof, *The Turning Point,* Simon and Schuster, New York, 1982, p. 361f

# I

## THE THEME

"What is the meaning of life?" The question is as old as mankind, and every answer is an interpretation of a world thick with enigmas. No answer is the final one, and none of them can answer the question completely. The answer changes as our knowledge of the world changes; meaning and unmeaning are part of the plenitude of life. "Life is crazy and meaningful at once. And when we do not laugh over the one aspect and speculate about the other, life is exceedingly drab, and everything is reduced to the littlest scale. There is then little sense and little nonsense either."[1] Jung wrote this at the age of fifty-nine. Twenty-five years later, the same thought acquires a strangely different intonation: "Which element we think outweighs the other, whether meaninglessness or meaning, is a matter of temperament. If meaninglessness were absolutely preponderant, the meaningfulness of life would vanish to an increasing degree with each step in our development. But that is—or seems to me—not the case. Probably, as in all metaphysical questions, both are true: Life is—or has—meaning and meaninglessness. I cherish the anxious hope that meaning will preponderate and win the battle."[2] In old age the question of meaning becomes a fateful one that decides the value or valuelessness of one's own life. Jung was profoundly stirred by it, yet he knew that there is no final or clear-cut answer.

It is the aim of this book to show what kind of "meaning"

Jung opposed to the "meaninglessness of life". Meaning for him was born of a long life, rich in experience, and of well over half a century of research into the human psyche. He found an answer that satisfied him, that tied up with his scientific knowledge though without claiming to be scientific. There is no objectively valid answer to the question of meaning; for, besides objective thinking, subjective valuation also plays its part. Each and every formulation is a myth that man creates in order to answer the unanswerable.

For Jung the question of meaning was not a philosophical or a theoretical problem. Like most themes in his work, it sprang from the daily experiences and necessities of the consulting hour. Jung was first and foremost a doctor, and the obligation to help and to heal remained decisive right up to the end of his life. The motto of his book *Answer to Job*,[3] "I am distressed for thee, my brother" (II Sam. 1:26), voices a powerful impetus behind his creativity and his thinking. The absence of meaning in life plays a crucial role in the aetiology of neurosis: "A psychoneurosis must be understood, ultimately, as the suffering of a soul which has not discovered its meaning."[4]

Jung records that "about a third of my cases are not suffering from any clinically definable neurosis, but from the senselessness and aimlessness of their lives."[5] They were not "sickly eccentrics" seeking from the doctor an answer to the question of meaning, "but . . . very often exceptionally able, courageous, and upright persons".[6] They were neurotic only because they shared what Jung called the "general neurosis of our time", an increasingly pervasive sense of futility. In most cases it went hand in hand with a sense of religious emptiness. These people were no longer able to believe, either because they could not reconcile scientific thinking with the tenets of religion, or because the truths enshrouded in dogma had lost authority for them and all psychological justification. If they were Christians, they did not feel redeemed by Christ's sacrificial death; if they were Jews, the Torah offered them no support. Thus they lacked the protection afforded by being rooted in a religious tradition. The man safely ensconced in religion will never entirely lose himself in the darkness and loneliness of a meaningless world, and in Jung's experience no one is really healed, and no one finds his meaning, "who did not regain his religious outlook. This of course has nothing whatever to do with a particular creed or membership of a church."[7]

As regards the question of life's meaning, no science can take the place of religion in this inclusive sense. Biological, physical, or cosmic systems of order no more provide an answer than does the interpretation of psychic contents exclusively in terms of personal experience. Meaning is the experience of totality. Any description of it presupposes the reality lived in time as well as life's quality of timelessness; personal and conscious experiences as well as a realm that transcends consciousness and the tangible world. If the tension between these two poles of being is lacking, man has the "feeling that he is a haphazard creature without meaning, and it is this feeling that prevents him from living his life with the intensity it demands if it is to be enjoyed to the full. Life becomes stale and is no longer the exponent of the complete man".[8] Life, for Jung, is lived only when it is "a touchstone for the truth of the spirit".[9]

# 2

## THE UNCONSCIOUS AND THE ARCHETYPE

*Hypothesis and Model*

The reality that transcends consciousness and appears as the spiritual background of the world is, in psychological terms, the unconscious. For this reason we must direct the attention of the reader not familiar with Jung's psychology to some of his theoretical statements concerning the unconscious and its contents, the archetypes. They form the basis for an understanding of the chapters to follow.

Jung was less concerned with the relatively limited sphere of the repressed and forgotten, which he called the "personal unconscious", than with the psychic background, the world of the "collective unconscious", he had discovered, or rather — seen in historical perspective — rediscovered.[1] (Whenever we speak of the "unconscious" in what follows, it is always the "collective unconscious" that is meant.) Unlike the personal conscious, it is a boundless realm that remains hidden because it is not connected with the ego-consciousness. "The marvellous thing about the unconscious is that it is really unconscious," he was fond of saying, and "the concept of the unconscious *posits nothing*, it only designates my *unknowing*" (Letter, February 1946).

The collective unconscious is not accessible to direct observation. But it can be investigated by an indirect and roundabout way, through the observation of conscious and therefore comprehensible contents that permits inferences to be drawn as to its nature and its structure. This methodical way was the one also taken by Freud, who, starting from the symptoms of hysteria, from dreams, parapraxes, jokes, etc., penetrated into the "concealment of the actual" (*Verborgenheit des Eigentlichen*) and inferred the unconscious as an unknown, hidden psychic realm. For Jung as well "the existence of an unconscious psyche is as likely, shall we say, as the existence of an as yet undiscovered planet, whose presence is inferred from the deviations of some known planetary orbit. Unfortunately we lack the aid of a telescope that would make certain of its existence".[2] The unconscious is an hypothesis.[3]

The way to building up the hypothesis was disclosed to Jung through the investigation of psychic images and ideas. Carefully he observed his own dreams and those of his patients; he analysed fantasies and delusions of the insane and engrossed himself in comparative religion and mythology. The decisive insight came to him from the fact that analogous images and myth motifs are to be found at all times and wherever human beings have lived, thought, and acted. From this "universal parallelism"[4] he inferred the presence of typical dispositions in the unconscious that are ingrained in man's make-up. As unconscious operators they constantly arrange the contents of consciousness everywhere in accordance with their own structural form, thus accounting for the similarity of the imagery. Jung called these inner dispositions or propensities *archetypes*, and characterised the conscious contents and motifs arranged by them as *archetypal*.[5]

The word *archetype* comes from the Greek; it means the "prime imprinter". With respect to manuscripts it denotes the original, the basic form for later copies.[6] In psychology archetypes represent the patterns of human life, the specificity of man. As they are unconscious quantities, they themselves remain irrepresentable and hidden, but they become indirectly

B

discernible through the arrangements they produce in our
consciousness: through the analogous motifs exhibited by
psychic images and through typical motifs of action in the
primal situations of life—birth, death, love, motherhood,
change and transformation, etc. The archetype *per se* stands like
a "producer" behind the archetypal motifs, but only these are
accessible to consciousness.

At various times archetypal motifs have emerged from the
unconscious make-up of man, and they can spontaneously
arise again at any time, anywhere, from the same dispositions.
Even when religious or mythical images are transmitted by
migration or tradition the archetypes function as unconscious
propensities that "select" contents of extraneous origin,
assimilate and integrate them. Philosophically considered, the
archetype is not the *cause* of its manifestations, but their
*condition*.

In the course of time Jung broadened his concept of the
archetype. He recognised that it had also to be seen as the
unconscious creative foundation of abstract ideas and scientific
theories. "The greatest and best thoughts of man shape themselves upon these primordial images as upon a blueprint."[7] It
was the physicist Wolfgang Pauli who took up this theme and
pointed out the influence of archetypal ideas on the inception
of scientific theories. "As *ordering* operators and image-formers
. . . the archetypes thus function as the sought-for bridge
between sense perceptions and ideas and are, accordingly, a
necessary presupposition even for evolving a scientific theory
of nature."[8] We shall come back to this in detail later on.

Jung's concept of the archetype is a continuation of traditional
Platonic thought. Just as for Plato the "idea", a kind of
spiritual model, is pre-existent and supraordinate to the
"appearance" or phenomenon, so for Jung is the archetype.

THE UNCONSCIOUS AND THE ARCHETYPE

" 'Archetype', far from being a modern term, was already in use before the time of St Augustine, and was synonymous with the 'Idea' in the Platonic usage."[9] Archetypes are "active, living dispositions, ideas in the Platonic sense, that preform and continually influence our thoughts and feelings and actions".[10]

Jung used the term archetype for the first time in 1919.[11] In his earlier writings we find instead the term "primordial image",[12] which he still occasionally employed later. This paraphrase proved to be not altogether a happy one. It led to misunderstandings, because "primordial image" was usually taken to mean something with a definite content, an "image" in fact, whereas according to Jung's definition it is unconscious as such and "irrepresentable". In analogy to the archetype "a primordial image is determined as to its content only when it has become conscious and is therefore filled out with the material of conscious experience".[13]

Other early designations for archetypes were "inherited path-ways"[14] and "deposits".[15] Jung supposed that these were produced in the course of generations as imprints of typical life experiences that recurred over and over again. Later he dropped these terms because they implied something that had gradually been built up, a specific content passed on by heredity, whereas he had come to see that archetypes are structural elements inherent in man's nature from the start. The archetype *per se* is timeless, it is "pure unvitiated nature".[16] Its origin is hidden from us and lies beyond the bounds of psychological and scientific knowledge. "Whether this psychic structure and its elements, the archetypes, ever 'originated' at all is a metaphysical question and therefore unanswerable."[17] The only thing that can be said with certainty is that they are inherited as irrepresentable dispositions in the unconscious, the timeless constants of human nature. On the other hand, the arrangements they produce (archetypal images and ideas) are formed anew in each individual life as time-conditioned variants of the timeless motif. The shaping of these variants depends equally on the unconscious disposition (the organising archetype), the environment, personal experience, and the given culture.

In order to illustrate the difference between the archetype *per se* and its manifestation as an archetypal image Jung liked to use the comparison of the crystalline grid present but indiscernible in the mother liquid (the unseen archetype *per se* in the unconscious, regulating the structural form), which first appears as a crystal according to the specific way in which the ions and molecules (the experimental material) aggregate. Each crystal actualises the basic structure of the grid, but in endlessly varied, individual form (the archetypal image in consciousness).[18]

"The archetype as such is a hypothetical and irrepresentable model.'[19] If Jung nevertheless introduced it as a concept into science and continually tried to apprehend its structure with greater precision, this was because—more particularly in his later, more differentiated formulations of it—he was out to construct a *model* that could be visualised. The construction of models in science is nothing out of the ordinary. Every science, when confronted with irrepresentable realities, is compelled to project models of them. The atom is in itself an entity that cannot be represented in time and space, but the physicist constructs a model of it from its observable effects. The biologist does the same thing in cases where he can study directly only the outside of the object, the inner processes of the organism remaining inaccessible to him.[20] This was what Jung did, too, when he constructed out of its observable effects a model of the archetype *per se*.

*The Archetype as Instinct and an Element of the Spirit*

In 1919, as we have said, Jung used the term archetype for the first time, when he also drew a comparison between the archetype as a structuring factor in the psychic realm, and *instinct* as an organiser of an *a priori* nature in the biological realm. He took as his starting-point "the incredibly refined instinct of propagation" in the South American yucca moth and the complicated ceremony of fertilisation it performs with the yucca plant. "The flowers of the yucca plant open for one night only. The moth takes the pollen from one of the flowers and kneads it into a little pellet. Then it visits a second flower, cuts open the pistil, lays its eggs between the ovules and then stuffs the pellet into the funnel-shaped opening of the pistil. Only once in its life does the moth carry out this complicated operation."[21]

Such mysterious processes in the animal world, unchanging and constantly repeated, are possible only because of the inborn instinct underlying them in the form of an unconscious disposition, an instinct which organises and shapes these processes as if it possessed a prior "knowledge". It is an innate, unconscious knowledge, refined down to the last detail, of the network of connections running through the world. In exactly the same way, archetypal motifs can be understood as expressing an *a priori* knowledge, a foreknowing of the behaviour appropriate in the primal situations of life. Archetype and instinct are unconscious factors that exert an ordering function. Therein lies their affinity: "To the extent that the archetypes intervene in the shaping of conscious contents by regulating, modifying, and motivating them, they act like the instincts."[22] From this it is but a short step to identifying the archetypes with "inherited, instinctive impulses and forms that can be observed in all living creatures".[23] In Jung's later writings instinct is often used alongside the analogous concept "pattern of behaviour".[24]

By characterising the archetype as an instinct or pattern of behaviour Jung described only one side of the model, namely its biological aspect. Its opposite pole is characterised with equal justification as the "authentic element of spirit".[25] As we have seen, the archetype acts as a kind of unconscious "knowledge", and furthermore it represents a "spiritual model" in the Platonic sense. Its "spirituality" is most clearly apparent in the immediate *experience* of its manifestations, "an experience of fundamental importance".[26] A man can be profoundly affected by an archetypal content, because its manifestation in consciousness radiates all the power of a numen. This numinous aspect "deserves the epithet 'spiritual' above all else".[27]

Jung uses the example of a Protestant theologian who dreamt repeatedly that he was standing "on a mountain slope with a deep valley below, and in it a dark lake. He knew in the dream that something had always prevented him from reaching the lake. This time he resolved to go to the water. As he approached the shore, everything grew dark and uncanny, and a gust of wind suddenly rushed over the face of the water. He was seized by a panic fear, and awoke."[28] "The dreamer descends into his own depths" is Jung's interpretation of the descent to the water. What seizes hold of him and throws him into a panic is hardly the dream image as such, for this is of the utmost simplicity: a gust of wind rushing over the lake. The numinosity of the image springs rather from the autonomous dynamism inherent in every archetype.[29] This manifests itself in the dream as the breath of the spirit, "which bloweth where it listeth". But, continues Jung, this is "uncanny, like everything whose cause we do not know—since it is not ourselves. It hints at an unseen presence, a numen to which neither human expectations nor the machinations of the will have given life. It lives of itself, and a shudder runs through the man who thought that 'spirit' was merely what he believes, what he makes himself, what is said in books, or what people talk about. But when it happens spontaneously it is a spookish thing, and primitive fear seizes the naïve mind".[30] And Jung goes on, not without a quizzical, sidelong glance at this pillar of theology: "Thus, in the dream, the breath of the pneuma frightened another pastor, a shepherd of the flock, who in the darkness of the night trod the reed-grown shore in the deep valley of the psyche."[31]

The fear bound up with such an experience is commonly the first reaction to an encounter with an archetypal content, which because of its autonomy, and perhaps also because of its strangeness, cannot be consciously accepted as a content of one's own psyche. But the archetype gets through in spite of the fear. "Often it drives with unexampled passion and remorseless logic towards its goal and draws the subject under its spell, from which despite the most desperate resistance he is unable, and finally no longer even willing, to break free, because the experience brings with it a depth and fullness of meaning that was unthinkable before."[32]

This brings us back to the initial question of *meaning*. The experience of meaning depends on the awareness of a transcendental or spiritual reality that complements the empirical reality of life and together with it forms a whole.[33] It is an experience that is expressed in the language of poetry as "All things ephemeral/Are but a reflection", and of religion as "the things which are seen are temporal, but the things which are not seen are eternal" (II Cor. 4:18). Psychologically, it is the recognition or experience of timeless archetypes as the hidden operators behind the scenes of life. In the passage above quoted, Jung is alluding to the central archetype of the *self*, of human wholeness.[34] It is that which "draws the subject under its spell" and finally brings with it "a depth and fullness of meaning", not only when this archetype is acknowledged as a transcendental power, but above all when life is devoted to its realisation. We shall come back to this point later.[35]

An experience of meaning, a spiritual happiness, is also granted to man in becoming conscious of new knowledge. According to Pauli this happiness, like understanding in general, seems to be "based on a correspondence, a 'matching' of inner images pre-existent in the human psyche with external objects and their behaviour".[36] This is a process that can take place even when man is not conscious of it.

### The Psychoid Archetype

The archetype is "an element of spirit", it is an instinct, "pure unvitiated nature"—such are the contradictory descriptions of it (or to be more precise, of its "model"). It must thus be thought of as a paradoxical entity. The setting up of paradoxes in science, even in the physical sciences, is nothing uncommon. A well-known example is the electron, which depending on the way it is observed behaves sometimes as a wave and sometimes as a particle. Though the observation of one reality rules out the observation of the other, both are valid. They supplement one another in the form of a complementarity. Dr Robert Oppenheimer speaks in this connection of a "duality" that applies to the nature of light and of all matter.[37] Duality, "the problem of opposites . . . that is profoundly characteristic of the psyche",[38] is true also of the contents of the unconscious. Fundamentally it is less a question of opposites than of antinomies, of self-complementing modes of manifestation.

In the course of the years Jung constantly attempted new formulations of the "idea" of the archetype and its projected "model" that would be truer to reality. The conception of its antinomy, however, not only remained intact but was given a deeper dimension. The final and crucial corrective, advanced in 1946, was the at first sight astonishing assertion that the "archetypes . . . have a nature that cannot with certainty be designated as psychic".[39] He drew this theoretical conclusion from the fact that the real nature of the archetype as a content of the collective unconscious remains unknowable, that it is a "metaphysical"[40] entity and as such not susceptible of any final or unequivocal definition. From then on he described it as "psychoid" or "quasi-psychic". "Psychoid" is an adjectival concept expressing the possibility of something being as much psychic as non-psychic. Whereas the archetypal model had up till then been described as an antinomy between instinct and spirit, its antinomy now reaches the most extreme tension imaginable between "spirit and matter" or "spirit and world". Previously Jung had been concerned with archetypal configurations in the realm of human thoughts, feelings, intuitions, etc. and in the realm of instinctive and organic life. The concept of the psychoid archetype added an altogether new dimension, for the possibility of an archetypal "imprinting" of the physical and inorganic world, and of the cosmos itself, had also to be taken into account.[41] Jung went even further and saw in the psychoid archetype the "bridge to matter in general".[42] The rigorous separation of psyche and world is abolished. In 1951 he wrote: "The deeper 'layers' of the psyche lose their individual uniqueness as they retreat farther and farther into the darkness. 'Lower down', that is to say as they approach the autonomous functional systems, they become increasingly collective until they are universalised and extinguished in the body's materiality, i.e., in chemical substances. The body's carbon is simply carbon. Hence 'at bottom' the psyche is simply 'world'."[43]

This new characterisation of the archetype as "psychoid",

with all the consequences this entails, is an audacious but quite logical extension of the original model of the archetype as an antinomian, paradoxical whole. Its far-reaching complementary aspects (as spirit and nature, as a structural element of the psyche and the world) explain its applicability in the humanities as well as in the natural sciences, and they also explain why depth psychology has a foot in both realms.

### Conscious Realisation as Discrimination

Consciousness is ruled by the psychological law that an unknown or unconscious content can be apprehended only by recognising its manifold aspects or by discriminating its opposite. In other words, discrimination of a single fact into two or more aspects, or the opposition between two contents, must be considered the prerequisite for any act of conscious realisation. We become conscious of "motion" by contrasting it with "rest", of "light" with "darkness", of "death" with "life", of "good" with "bad". "A being without opposites is completely unthinkable, as it would be impossible to establish its existence."[44] The corresponding law from the standpoint of the unconscious is: Once an archetype is made conscious, its paradoxicality falls apart and its latent opposites become manifest; only in this way can it emerge from the hidden recesses of the psychic background and be apprehended. Often this process of becoming conscious takes place by degrees. With contents that are not yet fully conscious their opposite aspects are still so close together that they cannot be clearly discriminated. That is why some dreams and fantasy figures appear so protean, contradictory, or paradoxical. In the fantasies of the alchemists the treasure they sought was a stone that is a spirit. Mercurius is a spirit and also quicksilver, an old man and a boy. At the beginning and end of the process there stands the dual figure of the hermaphrodite.

Nearer to consciousness and more easily grasped by it is the phenomenon of a pair of opposites in which two distinct figures belong together as complementary aspects of a single whole. In myths and fairy-tales such pairs appear as heaven and earth, sun and moon, hostile brothers, twins, angel and devil, tree of knowledge and tree of life, etc. In creation myths as well, the constituents and creatures of the world are brought into being as pairs of opposites: light and darkness, land and water, life and death, male and female.

Once the unconscious content is apprehended by consciousness, the pair is divided. The original parity of the opposites — the bipolar aspects of a single paradoxical archetype — retreats into a distance that consciousness can no longer reach. It is not even conceivable any more. How can spirit and nature be one? Or psyche and matter? In the place of prescient images of totality, veiled though they be from logical thought, there emerge clearly defined, independent concepts split off from it — a formidable achievement of human consciousness in its struggle to understand the world, yet fraught with the danger of psychic impoverishment through one-sidedness, and menaced by the loss of a unitary grasp of reality.

Thanks to the attention it pays to the unconscious as well as to consciousness, and thanks more particularly to its conception of the archetype as a psychoid, paradoxical entity, depth psychology takes its place among those sciences which today are working to produce a unitary picture of the world. This is the starting-point of Jung's answer to the question of meaning.

# 3

## JUNG'S METHOD AND STYLE

The development of the archetype concept in Jung's psychology may serve to illustrate the characteristics of his method of research. His work covers more than half a century of scientific exploration of a *terra nova*, the unconscious, and of the archetypes and their manifestations. Specific psychological questions crop up again and again, in early and in later writings. Each time the answers are thought through afresh, verified and reformulated, and sometimes use is made of new concepts. Jung often circled round the problems for years until he had felt his way through to his final answer and the problem seemed to him put in order and clarified. "First I made the observations, and only then did I hammer out my views."[1] That is the way of the pioneer. Strictly speaking the observations were not the prime thing. Behind them hovered an image, an archetype, one is almost tempted to say a vision, which step by step was brought nearer to reality. Jung spared himself no intellectual effort in amplifying his studies and observations until the image in his mind was buttressed up objectively, and was corrected and corroborated by factual evidence from without and within. This method is characteristic of the intuitive: his initial "hunch" becomes a creative insight when reinforced by the counter-function of sensation, the perception and observation of empirical facts. It is possible to follow out in Jung's work exactly how novel ideas, intuitions or hypotheses, which to begin with were cautiously introduced with the proviso "it may be conjectured" or "it seems to me", gradually condensed into solidly based scientific views.

The formulations and conclusions found in the early stages of this *longissima via* are neither false nor valueless. Seen in the perspective of the later writings, they are only provisional; not everything has yet been taken into account, and much has still to be recognised. This kind of development lies in the very nature of the material. The "ultimate" conclusions of science are always the last but one. The science of tomorrow will modify them, complete them, reformulate them or arrive at new insights. Even the meaning of the concepts changes.

Jung omitted to compare his early formulations with the later ones, and he did not always delimit the meaning of a concept he used from the meaning other writers had assigned to it. He was no systematiser, and it cannot escape the attentive reader of his work that the application of concepts and terminology is not always carried through consistently, that occasional contradictions and obscurities arise. These defects are due only in part to the impelling force of the creative daemon driving relentlessly forward. Scientific research was for Jung, as he himself admitted, not only an affair of the intellect, but was forced upon him by his own experiences and those of his patients. It was "a struggle, often a bitter one".[2] "Hence not everything I bring forth is written out of my head, but much of it comes from the heart also, a fact I would beg the gracious reader not to overlook if, following up the intellectual line of thought, he comes upon certain lacunae that have not been properly filled in."[3]

The attitude of the researcher, who was at the same time a doctor and helper, was supported by insight into the enigmas of the psyche. Though the psyche can be captured in any number of concepts and images it can never be wholly grasped. When the collective unconscious is at work, the conceptual statements of the psychologist are valid as definite truths only within certain limits. Beyond those limits he often has to make do with approximations and paradoxes. That is why the figurative or even poetic formulations one constantly comes across in Jung's work are sometimes more apt and closer to the truth than clear definitions. "The psyche is part of the inmost mystery of life."[4] Any statement that pays no heed to the mystery of the psyche is false from the scientific standpoint. In nuclear physics, which, like the psychology of the unconscious, is brought up against irrepresentable factors, there is, according to Niels Bohr, "a complementarity between the clarity and the rightness of a statement, so much so that a statement which is too clear always contains something false. Bohr's wish scrupulously to avoid anything not right moved him to a conscious renunciation of excessive clarity."[5]

Observations of psychic phenomena formed the basis of Jung's researches. The laws and connections he discovered in this way are remarkably consistent throughout his work. The occasional lack of uniform terminology, of clear formulation or precision, is not indeed cancelled out by this, but it nevertheless loses its importance in principle.

# 4

## THE HIDDEN REALITY

### Ordering Factors in Nature

The hypothesis of an unconscious underlying consciousness is the hallmark of psychological research in this century. Almost simultaneously, the natural sciences framed the corresponding hypothesis of a hidden reality underlying the phenomenal world. This gave rise to hitherto unrecognised analogies between the natural sciences and psychology, of which we shall cite a few examples.

Werner Nowacki, in his "Die Idee einer Struktur der Wirklichkeit",[1] begins with the structure of crystals, which is formed by different combinations of "elements of symmetry". These elements—there are thirty-two of them in all—are not material but abstract or even "spiritual" entities which have a formative effect. Nowacki calls them "primordial images". "One could," he writes, "regard them as irrepresentable formal factors that arrange the planes of the crystal as the material datum in a meaningful way that conforms to law", and that first manifest themselves visibly in this arrangement. He compares the elements of symmetry to archetypes and emphasises the significant analogy of their respective functions. Significant, because it turns out that both psyche and matter are structured or arranged, in accordance with corresponding laws, by invisible formal factors, these same "primordial images". The individual crystals, the concretisation of the elements of symmetry, can

assume various forms, just as in the psychic realm the archetypal configurations are endless variations of the archetype
*per se*. In Jung's words: "The archetype in itself is empty and
purely formal, nothing but a *facultas praeformandi* . . . our comparison with the crystal is illuminating inasmuch as the axial
system determines only the stereometric structure but not the
concrete form of the individual crystal. This may be either
large or small, and it may vary endlessly by reason of the
different size of its planes or by the growing together of
two crystals. The only thing that remains constant is the axial
system, or rather, the invariable geometric proportions underlying it. The same is true of the archetype. In principle, it can
be named and has an invariable nucleus of meaning—but
always only in principle, never as regards its concrete manifestation."[2]

In biology it was principally Adolf Portmann who drew
attention to the relation between the visible life of nature and
hidden "operators" or structural forms.[3] "Formation and new
formation in the realm of living organisms are not a production
of order out of a disordered chaos, they are the production of
order out of an already given, ordered structure."[4] With the
help of numerous examples from animal life—the migratory
flight of birds, the fight between viper and mouse, the relation
between butterfly and flower, the multiplication of unicellular
radiolaria—Portmann shows "how exactly this anticipated
structure of behaviour corresponds to something archetypal
which depth psychology finds also in man".[5] Particularly
impressive confirmation is afforded by the experimental
observation of blackcaps, which from the moment of hatching
were reared singly in complete isolation, far from any contact
with their kind. Each caged bird was put in a different place
in the open each night, and at the time of the migratory flights,

with moonless sky and clear stars, an agitated fluttering of the
birds could be observed, the attempts at flight being always in
the usual direction taken during their migration. Apparently
the blackcaps, even in captivity, oriented themselves by the
hereditary direction of the journey. Further experiments in a
planetarium, where the artificial starry sky was presented in
changing positions, not only corroborated this strange behaviour
but also explained it: it is the image of the starry sky with its
constellations that contains the direction-finding factors. Since
the birds were isolated there could be no question of behaviour
learnt or imitated, so one must conclude that an image of the
starry sky is inborn in the blackcap and that the orientation of
the migratory flight depends on this image—a wonderful
arrangement of organic life which prompted Portmann to ask:
"Would any defenders of the idea that the relation to the world
rests on an archetypal foundation ever have let his fantasy soar
to such flights of conjecture?"[6]

In the case of such instinctive arrangements it is a question,
as with the archetypes, of inborn, invisible triggering systems
which give biological processes a structure and put life "at the
ready". Portmann traces them back to a "primal ground of
unknown data" from which our own behaviour also originates,
since equally unknown data, the archetypes, shape our conscious experiences and actions.[7] The investigation of instincts
has led biology into a region it can no longer apprehend
scientifically. It is a "non-spatial abyss of mystery" which
opens out behind the living organism, or at its origin, and
which, as Portmann says, man encounters again and again in
examining his spiritual activity.[8] He also hints that the
"primal ground of unknown data" lying behind biological
events on the one hand, and the psychic hinterland, the unconscious, on the other, may be one and the same irrepresentable
mystery.

c

Physics also, in its more recent researches, has postulated a transcendental and autonomous "order" which acts formatively not only on matter but on the mind of man. "Somehow we shall not be able to avoid the conclusion," writes the theoretical physicist Walter Heitler, "that something spiritual also exists outside us, a spiritual principle which is connected both with the laws and events of the material world and with our spiritual activity . . . This leads us to the borders of metaphysics."[9] Pauli speaks of the "postulate of a cosmic order independent of our choice and distinct from the world of phenomena", or, more precisely, "an order thought to be objective, to which both the psyche of the perceiver and that which is recognised in the perception . . . are subject."[10]

The proof of such an order is supplied, for instance, by mathematics. Mathematics is a spiritual creation of man, yet it has sometimes been shown that the complicated mathematical laws discovered by him subsequently found their field of application in the processes and behaviour of external nature. For example, it has been established that planetary orbits obey the laws of an exceedingly abstruse geometry which man had discovered and worked out independently of astronomical observations. This seems most astonishing and can be satisfactorily explained only by postulating "an independent, objective order" that "imprints" both man and nature, or human thinking and the cosmos. "Classical physics with the complicated mathematical laws it operates with," writes Heitler, "has already forced us to conclude that our mind is somehow intimately connected with this external world, a connection which perhaps alone permits us to recognise these laws."[11]

Among the physicists it was Pauli who constructed the bridge to the psychology of the unconscious, using for this purpose the concept of the psychoid archetype. According to

Pauli the intimate connection between the human mind and the external world (left unexplained by Heitler's "somehow") is due to the fact that our ideas are arranged in an orderly manner by these archetypes. As psychoid structural elements they are the vehicles of that autonomous and transcendental order, "thought to be objective", which unites mind and world. They function, to repeat Pauli, "as the sought-for bridge between sense perceptions and ideas and are, accordingly, a necessary presupposition even for evolving a scientific theory of nature. However, one must guard against transferring this *a priori* of knowledge into the conscious mind and relating it to definite ideas capable of rational formulation."[12] With reference to the absence today of a unitary view of the world, Pauli stipulates that "the investigation of scientific knowledge directed outwards should be supplemented by an investigation of this knowledge directed inwards. The former process is devoted to adjusting our knowledge to external objects; the latter should bring to light the archetypal images used in the creation of our scientific theories. Only by combining both these directions of research may complete understanding be obtained."[13]

For Jung, one clue to the existence of a transcendental unity of psyche and world was afforded by so-called "extrasensory perceptions" (dreams that come true, clairvoyance, precognition, etc.) which are the subject matter of para-psychological research, the "border country between physics and psychology".[14] In these phenomena, for instance, an external event inaccessible to sense perception is nevertheless experienced as an internal event (say in a dream or an intuition). Both events, often widely separated in time and space, can be understood as arrangements produced by one and the same archetype. Its psychoid unity is in the process of splitting apart so that it appears here as a physical and there as a psychic reality.[15] We shall come back to this in greater detail later.[16]

### Science and Religion

A picture of the world built only on immediately discernible external facts no longer satisfies science today. Even metaphysical concepts like the hidden "ground of being" and spiritual structural elements, and metapsychical ones like the psychoid archetype, are included within it as co-determining factors. This marks a break with the intellectual tradition that has dominated science since the seventeenth century. It was then that the physical sciences developed quantitative thinking and brought about that rupture between the scientific and the metaphysical or religious view of the world which is characteristic of modern times.[17] In the centuries that followed, the paths of science and religion drew further and further apart. This had the initial advantage that investigators were able to work in the greatest freedom, and our knowledge of nature plumbed depths undreamt of before. The physical sciences, with technology in their wake, conquered the world. Yet this tremendous upsurge of technological achievement, still advancing irresistibly today, was not won without loss. The cosmos became as it were desouled, and natural phenomena were robbed of their spirituality. More and more the biological and physical aspects were taken for absolute reality, and the materialistic and mechanistic tendencies of science put the dignity of man as a spiritual being in question. In the face of this one-sidedness it is all the more significant that science today is once again confronted with the reality of a spirit operating autonomously and finds itself placed on the frontiers of metaphysics.

"In exploring the macrocosm [man] comes at last to a final featureless unity of space-time, mass-energy, matter-field—an ultimate, undiversified, and eternal ground beyond which there appears to be nowhere to progress," writes Lincoln Barnett.[18] From this prospect it is but a short step to the religious view. "Standing midway between macrocosm and microcosm," Barnett continues, "he finds barriers on every side and can perhaps but marvel, as St Paul did nineteen hundred years ago, that 'the world was created by the word of God so that what is seen was made out of things that do not appear'."[19] The religious echo is plainly audible in James Jeans: "The spirit no longer appears to us an intruder in the realm of matter; we begin to suspect that we should rather welcome it as the creator and ruler of the material realm",[20] and Heitler's postulate of an autonomous and regulating "spiritual principle existing outside us" comes very close to what we imagine a "divine principle" to be. Bernhard Bavink puts it simply and succinctly in his formulation: "Fundamentally, the pursuit of physics means nothing less than counting up God's elementary creative acts." Bavink wrote these words in 1948, in a book significantly titled *Die Naturwissenschaft auf dem Wege zur Religion* ("Science on the Way to Religion").

As we have seen, biology too has reached the frontiers of metaphysics. Portmann's concept of an invisible "abyss of mystery" containing the structural elements of life, of an "immense, unknown realm of the mysterious", can be understood only as a paraphrase for a religious content, a paraphrase that comes close to the theological description of God as the "ground of being".

During the last few years the most important investigators of nature have expounded their views of the world and set down their religious thoughts. The majority of them—and they include Einstein, Heisenberg, von Weizsäcker, Oppenheimer, Bohr, Jeans, and Heitler—address themselves not only to their professional colleagues but primarily to laymen seeking an answer to their questions. The large number of editions these publications have gone through shows that there is a widespread need to learn more about the religious and spiritual aspects of scientific research. It may be that this interest betokens a readiness to drop the prevalent one-sided materialistic picture of the world in favour of a more unified view and to give currency again to the religious and spiritual factors on a new plane. If this assumption is correct—and the present situation bears it out—there would seem to be some truth in the old saying that the first sip from the beaker of knowledge separates man from God, but that at the bottom of the beaker God waits for those who seek him.[21]

Obviously it is no longer a question today of reverting to the mediaevalistic attitude of mind and of throwing science and scientific thinking overboard. "The time, however, is ripe," says Heitler, "for us to become conscious of the metaphysical questions lurking behind the laws of nature, even if we cannot solve them at present or as (scientists) do not set out to solve them. But at any rate we should cease to offer as a 'world picture' that senseless, quantitative, deterministic machine which is presented today as the result of scientific research."[22] Jung was one of the first in this century to reject that senseless, quantitative, deterministic machine and to strike out on new ways of thinking and exploration. The collective unconscious he introduced into psychology is a "transcendental abyss of mystery" containing the archetypes as invisible ordering factors. It is an autonomous principle operating "outside us", that is, outside our conscious world, an "ultimate, undiversified, and eternal ground". Yet Jung's conception differs from that of physical scientists in that he did not limit the unconscious or the archetype to being exclusively a "spiritual principle". As we have seen, his researches and reflections led him to the view that both are "psychoid", and this implies that they are of a paradoxical nature which is both material and spiritual. Nor is psychology concerned solely with a connection between the transcendental principle and man's spiritual activity of theory-building; rather, the total man is exposed to the autonomous workings of the psychoid unconscious. As archetypal "patterns" they exert an ordering effect on his thinking and knowledge as well as on his psychic and biological life. They are the existential substrate of the total man and of the way he lives.

### The Numinosity of the Unconscious

The postulate of a transcendental spiritual order has brought the physical sciences face to face with the religious factor. The same is true of the psychology of the unconscious: the manifestations of the transconscious psyche and of the archetypes, to which we must now turn, bring with them an aura of numinosity and are described as experiences of a religious nature. In both realms the numinosity emanates from the autonomy of the hidden "operator": the spiritual principle postulated by the physical scientists is beyond human control, and in the archetypes there seems to be an immanent intentionality which the conscious mind experiences as a superior force, as something "wholly other" and strange, and even as hostile.

As an example of the autonomous workings of the unconscious, Jung often cited the story of the patient who was plagued by a severe anxiety neurosis. He suffered from an imaginary carcinoma, although the best doctors had assured him over and over again that he was perfectly healthy.[23] The patient knew quite well that the doctors were right, yet the "wholly other" proved stronger than the objective medical truth and his own reason. The anxiety always returned. What daemonic force was at work here? Who was chastising him with this deadly fear? Psychotherapeutic treatment was able to raise the unconscious psychic and religious background of his fear to consciousness, whereupon the tormenting chimaera vanished.

The little-known cases of people undergoing visionary experiences at the point of death often reveal the numinosity of the unconscious and its dynamism. Here is an example: After suffering several strokes, a woman of eighty-four, with a highly differentiated personality, was left in a state of physical helplessness and mental derangement. She no longer recognised anybody, not even her children. A few days before she died, she seemed to awake from a profound coma. She pointed to the corner of the room and said quietly and clearly: "There, look, there is the Holy!" And after a while: "It has been with me for hundreds of years. Holy, holy, holy." As she sank into unconsciousness again, her lips went on shaping the word "holy".

What happened here was all the more impressive because the dying woman was a down-to-earth person turned towards the realities of this world, who had shown hardly any interest in religious or psychological questions. But now the unconscious broke through as an autonomous agency with its timeless contents. In these and similar experiences[24] the ego or what remains of it, sinking into the unconscious, seems to be confronted with images that are outside the control of the will, the intensity and magnificence of which are utterly inconceivable in the normal state of consciousness. Even an observer who experiences them only indirectly is gripped by their numinosity.

The unconscious is a hidden, transcendental realm of being, an unknowable reality. That is why we cannot apprehend its workings and its powers directly. As they are autonomous, man cannot control them, "nor can he free himself or escape from

them, and therefore he feels them as overpowering".[25] It is
their overpoweringness that lends them numinosity and that
compels man to describe them as divine. "Recognising that
they do not spring from his conscious personality, he calls
these powers mana,[26] daemon,[27] or God. Science employs the
term 'the unconscious', thus admitting that it knows nothing
about it, for it can know nothing about the substance of the
psyche when the sole means of knowing anything is the psyche.
Therefore the validity of such terms as mana, daemon, or God
can be neither disproved nor affirmed. We can, however,
establish that the sense of strangeness connected with the
experience of something apparently objective, outside the
psyche, is authentic . . . Hence I prefer the term 'the unconscious', knowing that I might equally well speak of 'God'
or 'daemon' if I wished to express myself in mythic language.
When I do use such mythic language, I am aware that 'mana',
'daemon' and 'God' are synonyms for the unconscious—that is
to say, we know just as much or as little about them as about
the latter. People only *believe* they know much more about them,
and for certain purposes that belief is far more useful and
effective than a scientific concept."[28]

This passage comes from Jung's memoirs. It recapitulates and
sums up what he has said in numerous writings and verified
from empirical material. In the retrospect of the memoirs, it
distils the essence of his religious experience and of his
investigation of religious phenomena.

It would nevertheless be a mistake if the impossibility of
distinguishing between "God" and "the unconscious" led one
to infer from their synonymity that Jung predicated or assumed
their identity. This is one of the commonest misunderstandings
levelled against his psychology of religion. The indistinguish-
ableness refers only to the experience, not to that which is
experienced. In Jung's careful formulation: "This is certainly

not to say that what we call the unconscious is identical with God or is set up in his place. It is simply the medium from which religious experience seems to flow. As to what the further cause of such experience may be, the answer to this lies beyond the range of human knowledge. Knowledge of God is a transcendental problem."[29] Although God and the unconscious cannot be distinguished in our subjective experience, as self-subsistent entities they cannot be assumed to be identical. What does emerge from the unfathomableness of both God and the unconscious is the synonymity of the two concepts.

## Appearance and Reality

The distinction insisted on by Jung between that which is subjectively experienced or perceived (the archetypal content in consciousness) and that which subsists in itself (the archetype *per se*) characterises the epistemological foundation of his work from its beginnings. Time and again he referred to Kant and his *Critique of Pure Reason*, which states that "there can be no empirical knowledge that is not already caught and limited by the *a priori* structure of cognition".[30] Jung saw in Kant's theory of categories a renascence of the Platonic spirit.[31]

The modern physicist admits the same epistemological limitations, particularly since the researches into subatomic processes. In a passage that has become famous, Heisenberg declares that "we can no longer consider in themselves those building-stones of matter which we originally held to be the ultimate objective reality. This is because they defy all forms of objective location in space and time, and since basically it is always our knowledge of these particles alone which we make the object of science . . . the object of research is no longer nature, but nature exposed to human questioning. Here, again, man confronts himself alone."[32] Likewise C. F. von Weizsäcker: "Man tries to penetrate into the factual truth of nature, but in her last, unfathomable reaches suddenly, as in a mirror, he meets himself."[33]

Man can observe neither God, nor nature, nor the unconscious "in themselves". "We are fully aware that we have no more knowledge of the various states and processes of the unconscious as such than the physicist has of the process underlying physical phenomena. Of what lies beyond the phenomenal world we can have absolutely no idea . . ."[34] The only thing of which we have immediate knowledge is the psychic image reflected in consciousness. "To the extent that the world does not assume the form of a psychic image, it is virtually non-existent."[35]

The "objectivability of nature"[36] fails when it comes to observing the atom. It is no longer possible to speak of the behaviour of an atomic particle independently of the process of observation,[37] any more than we can speak of the behaviour of the unconscious independently of the observer. As in nuclear physics observation alters the behaviour of the particles, so in psychology "the archetype is altered by becoming conscious and being perceived, and it takes its colour from the individual consciousness in which it happens to appear".[38] "Between the conscious and the unconscious there is a kind of 'uncertainty relationship', because the observer is inseparable from the observed and always disturbs it by the act of observation."[39] The same is true of all the humanities and the social sciences: here as well the observation of particular processes is restricted by the uncertainty relationship. Even the science of history is incapable of telling us "what really happened", for again subject and object, observer and observed, are not completely separated.[40] For this reason history, as Theodor Lessing (1872-1933) puts it, is the "assignment of meaning to the meaningless". Niels Bohr's statement that "the present situation in physics is a forcible reminder of the old truth that we are as much spectators as protagonists of the great drama of existence"[41] can be applied with equal right to the present situation of the humanities and social sciences, and above all the psychology of the unconscious.

From the beginning, Jung concentrated on the analysis and interpretation of what presents itself to us as knowledge, as appearance, as a psychic image, knowing quite well that the "transcendental reality" beyond "the world inside and outside ourselves . . . is as certain as our own existence"[42] but nevertheless remains an unfathomable mystery. Hence the indistinguishability of God and the unconscious applies merely to the subjective experience and so has to be considered in interpreting the spontaneous religious assertions of individuals and in analysing myths and dogmas. In religious experiences too "man meets himself", or rather, he meets the self. The distinction between appearance (the subjectively experienced psychic image or content) and an "objective" reality hidden behind it calls for deepened insight and heightened consciousness. A new dimension is added to the experience by reflecting upon what has been experienced. Very often, however, this is felt as a loss of its immediacy or as a diminution and actual devaluation of its content, especially when this content pertains to the sphere of religion. The differentiation between the hidden reality and its appearance in consciousness formed for Jung the essential epistemological foundation of his psychological thinking and his work.

### The Numinosity of the Self

The relation of the psyche to religious reality does not depend only on the unconscious, the synonym for "God". Equally important is the fact that symbols of the self, the archetype representing the "essence of psychic wholeness", cannot be

distinguished from God-symbols.[43] The countless symbolisa-
tions of this totality of conscious and unconscious—Anthropos,
creator, father, mother, child, light, Word, trinity, quaternity,
circle, and so on—are also old and venerable God-symbols, and
when St Paul speaks of "Christ within me" (Gal. 2:20) God's
son must be taken in this sense as a symbol of the self, the
innermost core of the personality. Considering the indistinguishability of the concepts "God" and "unconscious" the
accent falls on the unknowable operator in the background, on
what the biologist calls the "abyss of mystery" and the
physicist the "spiritual principle". In the case of the indistinguishability of symbols of the self and God-images the
accent falls on the individual's relation to God.

The archetype of the self is symbolised in the psyche as an
*imago Dei*, a God-image, which no more than the unconscious
should be identified with God, let alone—a frequent misunderstanding—put in his place. In *Psychology and Alchemy* Jung
wrote: "Accordingly when I say as a psychologist that God is an
archetype, I mean by that the 'type' in the psyche. The word
'type' is, as we know, derived from τύπος, 'blow' or 'imprint';
thus an archetype presupposes an imprinter."[44] The "imprinter" is not touched on in Jung's work: "We simply do not
know the ultimate derivation of the archetype any more than
we know the origin of the psyche."[45] Jung does not by any
means set a negative valuation on the limitation of man's
capacity for knowledge, for in the end it is grounded in a
reality transcending man and life and therefore inapprehensible.
Thus "psychology . . . reserves the right to the poverty, or the
riches, of *not* knowing about the self".[46] It directs its attention
not to the imprinter, not even to the self as such, but confines
its investigations to the imprint, to the manifestations
arranged by the archetype in the human psyche. Even the self

is a model constructed by the psychologist only from its effects. The fact that psychology has demonstrated the numinous character of archetypal phenomena and their affinities with religious statements is one of its most impressive achievements.

### A Kabbalistic Parallel

God and the unconscious are synonymous concepts. Symbols of the self cannot be distinguished from God-symbols. These are two psychological discoveries of fundamental importance. In the first case it is something unknowable, and in the second case specific, knowable contents, that cannot be distinguished from God. In the history of religion this seeming contradiction has its parallel in myths of God as an ineffable and unfathomable being who at the same time is depicted by sacrosanct images and symbols regarded as valid. In the Jewish mysticism of the *Kabbala*, for example, statements that God is hidden, unknowable, and not to be named are coupled with countless vivid formulations of the divine being and with symbolic statements about clearly defined aspects of God. This juxtaposition forms one of the main themes of Gershom Scholem's *Major Trends in Jewish Mysticism*[47] and of his paper "Die mystische Gestalt der Gottheit in der Kabbala".[48]

The unfathomable hidden God "remains eternally unknowable in the depths of His own Self".[49] By his very nature he cannot—as an anonymous Kabbalist of the thirteenth century puts it—be the subject of any communication. Consequently, this Kabbalist goes on, he is nowhere hinted at in the earliest records of revelation, in the canonical books of the Bible and in Rabbinic tradition. Circumlocutions like "Root of all Roots", "Great Reality", "Undifferentiated Unity" are used as makeshifts for describing the indescribable. One of the most significant of these circumlocutions is to be found in the principal work of the older *Kabbala*, the *Zohar* ("Book of the Radiance", thirteenth century). There the highest designation of the hidden God is "En-Sof", which, surprisingly enough, must be translated not as "*He* who is Endless" but as "*That* which is Endless". By means of this neuter term Jewish mysticism guards against any personal nuance and any concretisation. In the writings of Isaac the Blind, the earliest of the Kabbalists who can be identified and who lived in Provence in the twelfth century, the hidden God is similarly said to be "*That* which is Ungraspable", not "*He* who is Ungraspable".

En-Sof, the endless, the ungraspable, is formless and unknowable. There are no images depicting it, no names naming it. The connection with the commandment in the Old Testament, not to make any likeness of God, is plain. Yet in Kabbalistic literature we find, besides the imageless hidden God, time-hallowed symbols of a God with form and shape. According to Scholem, God "is not only the formless abyss into which everything sinks, though he is that too; he contains in his outward emanation the guarantee of form".[50] The aspect of the hidden God reposing in himself, En-Sof, is complemented by the other aspect of a God pouring himself out in his emanations and, in his workings, turning to his creatures. In this aspect God is not formless and ungraspable, but has a "mystic garment", a shape that can be symbolically represented in names and images. The profoundest reflections and experiences of Kabbalistic mysticism are concerned with the formulation and elaboration of this shape.

A mysterious connection is preserved between the hallowed symbols of the divine being and the unnameable Ground. Paradoxically, the amorphous substance of En-Sof is directly present in the symbolic shapes of its divine emanations. Moreover it is present in every creature and in every shape that can possibly be imagined. The Kabbalistic idea is that

God's life pours out to animate the whole of creation; at the same time it remains hidden in his innermost depths. It is shapeless yet dwells in shapes. "The truer the shape, the mightier the life of the Shapeless dwelling within it."[51]

This brief sketch of the dualistic concept of God in the mysticism of the *Kabbala* is not without affinities with the scientific findings and formulations of Jungian psychology: there is a parallel between the hidden, amorphous, unknowable En-Sof and the unconscious. The unconscious, too (as a synonym for God) is hidden and unutterable, and the psyche is "one of the darkest and most mysterious regions of our experience".[52] The unconscious is "endless", no bounds can be assigned to it, and "it is altogether inconceivable that there could be any definite figure capable of expressing archetypal indefiniteness".[53] On the other hand the Kabbalistic symbol of the "garment of God", the multitudinous designations of his shape as a world-builder, correspond to the numinous symbols which depict the self as the archetype of creation and order and cannot be distinguished from God-images. En-Sof, hidden and endless, is contained in its entire reality in the images of God pouring himself into the world. Similarly, in the archetype of the self our limited consciousness is united with the unfathomable unconscious. It is a particle in which the whole dwells and works.

The analogies between religious ideas in Jewish mysticism that are hundreds of years old and the scientific findings of modern psychology can be explained only by the archetypal structure of the psyche. Man's images and ideas concerning the mysteries of being fall into the timeless patterns arranged by the archetypes in the unconscious; his meditations are determined by them. Within the setting of his culture and his time, he creates new forms for the expression of age-old truths. It seems significant that the religious genius of the Jewish mystics intuitively recognised the nature and limits of metaphysical knowledge and expressed them in paradoxes, and that the scientific attitude of the psychologist Jung is imbued with a genuine, indeed passionate feeling for religion. In the last resort, science and religion cannot be separated.

### A Theological Parallel (Paul Tillich)

The emphasis on the two aspects of divinity—infinite beyond understanding and finite in its historical and individual manifestations—also plays a role in modern theological thinking. In the religious world view of the German theologian Paul Tillich, who lived in the United States from 1933 until his death in 1965, an absolute but indefinable "God beyond God" stands behind every theistic God however defined by a religion or a creed. The "God beyond God" must "transcend the theistic objectivation of a God who is a being".[54] "Personalism with respect to God (must be) balanced by a transpersonal presence of the divine."[55] Tillich distinguishes between the "infinite source of all holiness" and a "finite holiness". Finite holiness finds expression in historical religions. The infinite source of all holiness, on the other hand, is "unconditioned" and inexpressible. Although it shines through the forms of finite holiness it must not be confused with this; for "wherever anything finite, whether it be a holy doctrine, a holy institution, a holy book, a holy person, a holy sect, is equated with the infinite source of all holiness, the finite holiness seeks to subordinate to itself everything else that is finite; it seeks to break all resistance to its absolute claim, and the first victim of this attempt is humanity".[56]

Jung's statements on religion meet Tillich's requirements. He remained aware of the human limitations of his knowledge, so that the human element never got lost and tolerance was taken for granted. "I see many God-images of various kinds,"

D

he wrote to a theologian (June 1955), "I find myself compelled to make mythological statements, but I know that none of them expresses or captures the immeasurable Other, even if I were to assert it did." And in his preface to *Answer to Job* he says: "If, for instance, we say 'God', we give expression to an image or verbal concept which has undergone many changes in the course of time. We are, however, unable to say with any degree of certainty—unless it be by faith—whether these changes affect only the images and concepts, or the Unspeakable itself."[57]

The agreement between Tillich's views and Jung's is evidence of a scientific attitude which, intentionally or otherwise, harks back to the old Platonic principles of thought in the investigation of religious contents.[58] Plato realised that we learn nothing about God from science, since our knowledge is limited. For him the One God beyond all being was an "unknown God". The mathematician Andreas Speiser therefore calls *"fratres in Platone"* all those who in religious questions follow not faith alone, but the scientific conscience, the "best legacy of the Hellenes", and who limit their statements accordingly. There aren't many of them, but they wander through the ages, "a small band of honest folk, the salt of the earth, occasionally protesting, often paying for their courage with their life".[59]

Jung followed his scientific conscience when he accepted religious statements not by faith alone but examined them for their archetypal content. This often earned him the reproach of "psychologism". The reproach would be justified only if he were speaking of God himself. In accordance with Platonic thinking his scientific work was concerned only with man's statements about God and the divine. They afforded him deep insight into the nature of the psyche. God himself remained inviolate. Yet the limitation he imposed on himself did nothing

to deny the existence of the "Unspeakable". "I do not by any
means dispute the existence of a metaphysical God," he wrote
to one of his critics (May 1952). "But I allow myself to put
human statements under the microscope." His researches into
the psychology of religion and his insights are grounded on
phenomenology and the way it interprets man's statements
about the divine and the numinous. "I am quite conscious that
I am moving in a world of images and that none of my reflections touches the essence of the Unknowable,"[60] is one of the
many formulations that mark out the boundaries of his
insights.

# 5

## INNER EXPERIENCE

*Alchemy as an Expression of Inner Experience*
The human statements that Jung "put under the microscope" include not only dreams and visions, myths and dogmas, but also the abstruse, and sometimes scurrilous, texts of alchemy. They became for him a treasure house of spontaneous religious utterances of the psyche. Alchemical treatises can be taken only in part as reports of chemical processes.[1] Jung came to see that the old Masters did not observe "objectively" the substances they attempted to investigate, as though they were modern chemists, but filled them with projections of unconscious psychic contents and images. This explains the mythical ideas and fairy-tale motifs which they associated with the elements and metals, and with the transformations these underwent in their alembics and crucibles. Projections of psychic contents are an everyday happening; they occur whenever a person is confronted with something strange that he does not understand —in this case matter. In his efforts to understand and describe the unknown substances, their combinations and dissolutions, the alchemist did not discover chemical compounds, or not these alone, but created a way for his psyche to express itself. The modern scientist who tries to penetrate into the elusive mysteries of nature finds himself in a similar situation. He too, as we have seen, is unable to consider the objects of his observation "in themselves". But unlike him, the alchemist still had no notion that in the darkness of matter he sought to

illuminate he would "suddenly, as in a mirror, meet himself". He was quite unconscious of the psychological background and the limitations of his knowledge.

Jung read the alchemical works, written in a language loaded with symbols, primarily as records of unconscious psychic processes and interpreted them as though they were dreams or visions.[2] He demonstrated that the treasures the alchemists sought in their manifold procedures yet never found — the gold, the philosophers' stone or "stone of the wise", the elixir, the red slave, the white woman, etc. — should not be understood only as chemical formulas but as archetypal, numinous images born of the psyche. They often bear a startling resemblance to the articles of the Christian religion which alchemy reflected as in a mirror. Thus, many qualities were attributed to the *lapis*, the goal of the alchemical opus, which represent it, in spite of its materiality and earthliness, as a parallel to the figure of Christ. It too is a redeemer and incorruptible, is spirit and body, is rejected and becomes the cornerstone, etc. The chapter entitled "The Lapis-Christ Parallel" in *Psychology and Alchemy* contains the key to an understanding of alchemical religiosity and its relation to Christianity. The archetypal images the alchemists projected into matter symbolise in ever renewed forms a spirit that was thought of not as a *son of light* but as the *son of matter* lying hidden in its darkness. Psychologically it must be interpreted as a "spirit in the unconscious".

The attitude of the serious adept was genuinely religious, and the most important of the philosophical alchemists confessed in their writings that the religious side of their "art" was the focus of their interest and endeavours — above all their inner experiences during the opus. Jung described the "arcane" philosophy of alchemy, which in the form of meditation and creative imagination went hand in hand with work in the laboratory, as "gnosis", an intuitive knowledge of God. From

the historical point of view he saw in it a continuation of early
Christian Gnosticism; while from the psychological standpoint
he found in the riches and profundities of alchemical imagery
proof and confirmation of the religious function of the psyche.

### The Unconscious as Inner Experience

The faculty of the psyche to create religious images seemed to
Jung to be one of its most wonderful properties. "It has the
dignity of an entity endowed with consciousness of a relationship to Deity. Even if it were only the relationship of a drop of
water to the sea, that sea would not exist but for the multitude
of drops."[3] The religious images produced by the psyche form
the basis of its relationship to the hidden Deity: "It would be
going perhaps too far to speak of an affinity; but at all events
the soul must contain in itself the faculty of relationship to
God, i.e., a correspondence, otherwise a connection could never
come about. *This correspondence is, in psychological terms, the archetype of the God-image.*"[4] In other words, the archetypal God-
image enables the soul "to be an eye destined to behold the
light";[5] for "as the eye to the sun, so the soul corresponds to
God".[6]

It cannot be overlooked that in comparing the soul to "God",
Jung did not adhere with due rigour to the epistemological
restriction he had imposed on himself, but was pointing to the
"Unspeakable itself". In the fervour of creation the *homo
religiosus* broke through the sober argument of the scientist.
All the same, this encroachment upon the realm of metaphysics and the emotion behind it lend these passages particular weight, and the reader has the advantage of being able to
grasp immediately what it is all about: everyone knows what
"God" is without knowing it. Jung himself was fully aware
of his occasional transgressions and provided an explanation:
"If we leave the idea of 'divinity' quite out of account and

speak only of 'autonomous contents', we maintain a position that is intellectually and empirically correct, but we silence a note which, psychologically, should not be missing. By using the concept of a divine being we give apt expression to the peculiar way in which we experience the workings of these autonomous contents."[7] In a letter (November 1959)[8] he justified the use of the concept "God" as a formulation of an autonomous agent: "I know, it is a matter of a universal experience and, in so far as I am no exception, I know that I have such experience also, which I call God. It is the experience of my will over against another and very often stronger will, crossing my path often with seemingly disastrous results, putting strange ideas into my head and manoeuvring my fate sometimes into most undesirable corners or giving it unexpected favourable twists, outside my knowledge and my intention. The strange force against or for my conscious tendencies is well known to me. So I say: 'I know Him.' But why call this something 'God'? I would ask: 'Why not?' It has always been called 'God'. An excellent and very suitable name indeed. Who could say in earnest that his fate and life have been the result of his conscious planning alone? Have we a complete picture of the world? Millions of conditions are in reality beyond our control. On innumerable occasions our lives could have taken an entirely different turn. Individuals who believe they are masters of their own fate are as a rule the slaves of destiny. A Hitler or Mussolini could believe they were such masterminds. *Respice finem!* I know what I want, but I am hesitant and doubtful whether that something is of the same opinion or not."

The inner certainty of the psyche's relationship to God is based on an archetypal experience to which religious and creative people in all ages have borne witness. In *Liber de*

*Spiritu et Anima* attributed to St Augustine (354–430), it is assumed that self-knowledge paves the way to knowledge of God.[9] We read in Meister Eckhart (1260–1329): "For the soul is created equal with God." And: "The soul is all things. It is so, because it is an image of God. But as such it is also the Kingdom of God."[10] In the last century Brahms (1833–79) called the "subconscious" a "spark of divinity". "All genuine inspiration comes from God, and He can reveal himself to us only through that spark of divinity within us—through what the modern philosophers call the subconscious."[11] Much the same thought is expressed by Ricarda Huch (1864–1947) in her interpretations of the Bible: "The womb from which the hidden goal within us strives towards fulfilment is now usually called the unconscious, whereas the Bible calls it God."[12] The Cretan poet Nikos Kazantzakis, who died a few years ago, summed up his inner and outer experiences and his quest for truth thus: "On earth and in heaven there is nothing more like God than the soul of man." These are the words with which he concludes the "report"[13] of his youth.

Jung has shown that the greatest help for modern man in his spiritual distress, his feeling of being lost in a meaningless world, his unfulfilled longings, and also his deceptive sense of well-being in a spiritual and religious void, is to be found in *inner experience*. Instead of the faith that has got lost, Jung demands of him a new and intense participation in religious life; for it should be obvious from what has been said that inner experience, the encounter with the figures of the unconscious, is a religious experience. This is the core of his psychology of religion. "It has yet to be understood that the *mysterium magnum* is not only an actuality but is first and foremost rooted in the human psyche."[14] *The encounter with the mystery of the psyche cannot be distinguished from an experience of God.*

Jung nevertheless leaves his reader in no doubt that the way to religious experience through the psyche is a hazardous one. Courage and inner strength are needed to pay serious attention to the voices and images that crowd into consciousness, to endure the encounter with the numinous figures, to understand them and take their meaning to heart. Only by holding out against it can one transform that by which one is oneself transformed. Just this is the task of modern man, as Jung saw it: "The spiritual adventure of our time is the exposure of human consciousness to the undefined and indefinable."[15] But the adventure is successful only when the descent into the unconscious changes from passive exposure into active participation. By taking up an attitude towards it, consciousness delimits itself from the unconscious, broadens its scope so that the personality can unfold.

Experience of the numinous unconscious is collective, yet it belongs to the most personal and intimate part of man. It is as personal as it is absolute. "It cannot be disputed. You can only say that you have never had such an experience, whereupon your opponent will reply: 'Sorry, I have.' And there your discussion will come to an end. No matter what the world thinks about religious experience, the one who has it possesses a great treasure, a thing that has become for him a source of life, meaning, and beauty, and that has given a new splendour to the world and to mankind. He has *pistis* [trust] and peace. Where is the criterion by which you could say that such a life is not legitimate, that such an experience is not valid, and that such *pistis* is mere illusion? Is there, as a matter of fact, any better truth about the ultimate things than the one that helps you to live? That is the reason why I take careful account — *religio!* —of the symbols produced by the unconscious."[16]

Only on one point did Jung express himself later with less positive conviction: a numinous experience is no guarantee of

inner peace, not in the long run anyway. So long as one continues to develop, inner peace, even for those whose life has been
enriched by an encounter with the unconscious, is only a breath-
ing-space between the conflict solved and the conflict to come,
between answers and questions that throw us into turmoil and
suffering, until new insights or new transformations bring a
fresh solution and the inner and outer opposites are once again
reconciled. The experience of meaning—which is what,
ultimately, life is about—is by no means equivalent to non-
suffering; yet the resilience of the self-aware and self-transforming consciousness can fortify us against the perils of the
irrational and the rational, against the world within and the
world without.

Even as a child, Jung was alert to the numinous effect of
archetypes. He experienced "God" as an overwhelming will at
work within him. He argued with it with all the gravity of a
child,[17] and felt its full impact in dreams and in powerful
fantasy images that aroused his reverence and fear. Looking
back, at the age of eighty-three he could say: "At that time I
realised that God—for me, at least—was one of the most
immediate experiences."[18] His definition that " 'God' is a
primordial experience of man"[19] is likewise a personal confession. Inner experience was his native element, far more so
and in a much profounder sense than for other people. With
this in mind Erich Neumann wrote: "Strangely unaware of his
own nature, Jung forgets that his experience is altogether out of
the ordinary, that in scope and content it transcends by far that
of his fellow mortals and on that account is rated 'mystical',
and must be so rated until they themselves have had this
experience of a more embracing reality hitherto unknown to
them."[20]

Only a few people have spontaneous experiences of God.

Jung wrote that he knew a few of them, and they were the very ones he had to accompany "through the crises of personal conflicts, through the panics of madness, through desperate confusions and depressions which were grotesque and terrible at the same time."[21] Recalling such encounters Jung often quoted in his later writings the words of St Paul: "It is a fearful thing to fall into the hands of the living God" (Heb. 10:31). Even a consciously undertaken descent into the unconscious and an active confrontation of its contents—which Jung called "active imagination"[22]— lead, if not always, but certainly in most cases, to an experience of the numinous.

Jung himself trod the path of this confrontation with the unconscious after his separation from Freud in 1912.[23] His object was to explore its deeper layers which Freud had either not seen or not been able to understand. So Jung embarked on the psychic adventure of exposing himself to the "undefined and indefinable". He was the first to do so and to go it alone with no inkling of where it would lead him. No terrors were spared him on this inner voyage of discovery; he has given an account of it in his memoirs. The confrontation lasted over four years (1912-16).

Understandably, readers who had never undergone any such experience found that Jung's autobiographical report brought them face to face with an utterly strange world. To the psychiatrists among them, it was known at most from the fantasies of the insane. The scientific results of this extraordinary and courageous undertaking were consequently overlooked, and neither psychiatrists nor laymen hesitated to insinuate, or to declare openly, that Jung was a schizophrenic or at any rate a latent schizophrenic. Forty-five years after his odyssey into the world of archetypal images, from which he returned richly laden with experience and insight, he offered a diagnosis and explanation of his adventures. This is to be found in the second part of his book *Mysterium Coniunctionis*, published in 1956, a few years before the memoirs. Jung himself compared the descent into the deeper layers of the psyche with a psychosis, but characterised this more specifically as an "anticipated psychosis". Because of its fundamental importance with regard to an immediate experience of the collective unconscious the passage is quoted here verbatim:

"Naturally there is an enormous difference between an anticipated psychosis and a real one, but the difference is not always clearly perceived and this gives rise to uncertainty or even a fit of panic. Unlike a real psychosis, which comes upon you and inundates you with uncontrollable fantasies erupting from the unconscious, the judging attitude implies a voluntary involvement in those fantasy-processes which compensate the individual and—in particular—the collective situation of consciousness. The avowed purpose of this involvement is to integrate the statements of the unconscious, to assimilate their compensatory content, and thereby produce a whole meaning which alone makes life worth living and, for not a few people, possible at all. The reason why the involvement looks very like a psychosis is that the patient is integrating the same fantasy-material to which the insane person falls victim because he cannot integrate it but is swallowed up by it. In myths the hero is the one who conquers the dragon, not the one who is devoured by it. And yet both have to deal with the same dragon. Also, he is no hero who never met the dragon, or who, if once he saw it, declared afterwards that he saw nothing. Equally, only one who has risked the fight with the dragon and is not overcome by it wins the hoard, the 'treasure hard to attain'. He alone has a genuine claim to self-confidence, for he has faced the dark ground of his self and thereby has gained himself. This experience gives him faith and trust, the *pistis* in the ability of the self to sustain him, for everything that menaced him from

inside he has made his own. He has acquired the right to
believe that he will be able to overcome all future threats by
the same means. He has arrived at an inner certainty which
makes him capable of self-reliance . . ."[24]

Here the confrontation with the perils and numinous
powers of the unconscious is compared to the mythical fight
with the dragon. It is an archetypal experience, as old as
humanity; the primordial experience of the divine as a *tremendum*, and of meaning as deliverance and redemption. In the
archaic imagery of myth, the human mind has given it an
expression that has never lost its universal validity.

It should be added in passing that by no means every confrontation with the unconscious leads to a life-and-death
struggle. Much depends on the individual's inner balance and
on the tension between the ego and the unconscious. If the
ego-personality is weak or narrow, or if the unconscious is
overwhelmingly powerful as a result of personal constitution
or the constellation of the moment, then consciousness is
indeed challenged to the extreme and a man's whole resources
are needed until he can liberate himself from the darkness and
terror of the struggle, and has found that "inner certainty
which makes him capable of self-reliance".

It should further be noted that in recent years psychiatrists have
begun to see schizophrenia in a new light, as an inner experience that is nature's own attempt at psychic healing in certain
insoluble or intolerable situations of life. It is a plunge into the
collective unconscious of which the so-called "normal" person
usually knows nothing. The Scottish psychiatrist R. D. Laing
therefore logically concludes that "schizophrenics have more to
teach psychiatrists about the inner world than psychiatrists
their patients".[25] According to Laing, schizophrenia may
sometimes be the behavioural expression of an "experiential

drama'', the "*forme frustre* of a potentially *natural* process, that we do not allow to happen because we are so busy 'treating' the patient, whether by chemotherapy, shock therapy, milieu therapy, group therapy, psychotherapy, family therapy — sometimes now, in the very best, most advanced places, by the lot".[26] He sees schizophrenia, in short, as an "initiation ceremonial",[27] a journey into the interior realms of the psyche. "The person who enters this inner realm (if only he is allowed to experience this) will find himself going, or being conducted . . . on a journey."[28] "Can we not see," he ends, "that this voyage is not what we need to be cured of, but that it is in itself a natural way of healing our appalling state of alienation called normality?"[29] "If the human race survives . . . they will see that what we call 'schizophrenia' was one of the forms in which, often through quite ordinary people, the light began to break through the cracks in our all-too-closed minds."[30]

Laing refers to Jung in a context which, unfortunately, is not altogether clear. "Jung broke the ground here, but few followed him."[31] These words leave one in doubt whether he is referring to Jung's publications on schizophrenia[32] or to his memoirs, where he describes not only his own "journey into the interior"[33] but the corresponding experiences of his patients.[34]

Laing does not omit, in conclusion, to raise the critical question: "What needs to be explained is the failure of many who embarked on this voyage to return from it."[35] He is inclined to see the cause of the failure in unfavourable external conditions of the patient's life which make a return seem implausible. But, psychologically considered, it might well be the other way round: the experience of the inner world may be so fascinating, and the contents of the collective unconscious so overpowering, that the ego-personality is held captive or even completely shattered by them, so that any prospect of healing comes to nothing. Such patients have succumbed to "the fate of Theseus and Peirithous, who descended into Hades and grew fast to the rocks of the underworld".[36]

In his memoirs Jung reports the case of an eighteen-year-old girl, a catatonic, who in her schizophrenic fantasies lived with the moon people. He succeeded in curing her, whereupon she reacted with violent resistances and reproaches: Jung had stopped her from returning to the moon, she could no longer escape from the earth. "This world was not beautiful, but the moon was beautiful, and there life was rich in meaning."[37]

So long as Laing's question about the return from the world of schizophrenic fantasies remains unanswered, there is still a wide field for further researches into schizophrenia and its aspect as a healing experience of the inner world. A different thing altogether from schizophrenia as a pathological illness from which the patient does not return is—let it be emphasised again—the experience of an "anticipated psychosis" whose healing power Jung tested. Here the ego-consciousness stands firm in its bouts with the numinous contents of the collective unconscious, so that the way back from the realm of inner experience to the world of consciousness, of one's fellow men, and of personal responsibility always remains open.

### Modern Art as an Expression of Inner Experience

"The spiritual adventure of our time is the exposure of human consciousness to the undefined and indefinable," we quoted Jung as saying.[38] This is as true of psychology, which includes the unconscious within the scope of its research and practical work, as of natural science in its confrontation with a transcendental background of being. And not only is this true of modern science as a whole, but the creations of "modern art" (if we may be permitted to use so generalising a term) also portray the history of an exposure of the human spirit to the undefined and indefinable—a sign of the collective significance of this "adventure". For, unlike science, art addresses itself to every man, and gives expression to the inner processes at work in him.

Artists were among the first in our century to risk an encounter with the unconscious and its indefinable background. In the early decades they tried, each in his own way, to get behind the façade of the phenomenal world.[39] "Appearance is eternally flat, but a daemon impels us artists to look between the cracks of the world, and in dreams he leads us behind the wings of the world's stage." Thus Franz Marc formulated the longing for an existential reality behind appearances. Driven by fate, a whole crowd of artists followed the way within; in their work they sought to express a "higher and profounder condition of being" (Carlo Carrà). Kandinsky, perhaps the most important theoretician among those artists, demanded: "The artist's eye should always be turned in upon his inner life, and his ear should always be alert for the voice of inward necessity." With the evocation of the "inner life" the unconscious debouched into art: the unfathomable, invisible background of the living world is the "secretly perceived that has to be made visible" (Paul Klee). After an epoch of concentration on form and nature in the realism and impressionism of the nineteenth century, this was indeed a bold departure, a new and unprecedented interpretation of the theme of art. It was a turning-point that had its parallel in the natural sciences, which about that time began to get over the materialism of the nineteenth century.

Gripped by their inner vision and endeavouring to give shape to "that secret ground where primal law feeds growth" (Klee), to capture the "metaphysical aspect of things" (Chirico), the "changeless reality behind changing natural forms" (Mondrian), artists turned their backs more and more on the reality of the external world. Their pictures became non-objective, abstract, imaginative, or else the object was transmuted in terms of subjective inner experience, sometimes lifted into the archetypal realm, sometimes perverted into absurdity. Their countless attempts to outline in manifestoes their pictorial goal show clearly that what was at stake was far more than a new style or a new formal or aesthetic technique. They were attempts to penetrate to the hidden spirit of nature and of things, to disclose the background of life, to portray an inner reality, to express the irrational, so as to gain access to a new, vital centre. Artists were seized by the numinosity of the unconscious, art had become mysticism. They were trying to "express the mystic vision", as Kandinsky put it. Like the scientists, they were brought face to face with the religious question, the question of an active, transcendental spirit.

Naturally the mysticism of the art movements starting at that time had nothing in common with the contents and aims of Christian mysticism, nor had the spirit from which they arose anything to do with the Christian spirit. On the contrary, the spirit that permeated the "mystical inner construction" (Franz Marc) with the interplay of colour and form, and got on to the canvas as a "mystic vision", was totally alien to the spirit of Christianity and Christian culture. Hence the feeling of something novel and revolutionary, and the need to break with artistic tradition. It was a spirit that burst out of the unconscious, and was described by the pioneers of modern art as the spirit of things, creatures, matter, nature—in short, a chthonic spirit, alien and opposed to the spirit of Christianity, and one which from the psychological point of view might be regarded as its compensation. It found adequate expression in fantasies and abstractions, scurrilous or brutal forms, visions, sculptures, paintings, collages, and irrational configurations made of stone, wood, metal, glass, and even of junk (Schwitters).

E

Looked at historically, the chthonic spirit that informs modern art is age-old. Its mythological personifications go back to the pagan religions of antiquity, when it played a significant role as a nature deity. After Christianity had transformed the pagan consciousness it met with opprobrium and could no longer be expressed in adequate form. To the Christian consciousness, oriented to a "heavenly" spirit, it was something that had to be conquered because of its darkness, bound as it was to earth, nature, and the world of things. It was repressed and sank into the unconscious. But this rejection changed its nature and its appearance: it became evil and ugly. As history shows, its ghost has never been completely laid, but lives on in the depths, unrecognised, as the Doppelgänger of consciousness through the centuries. As a negative, destructive spirit it breaks through in the well-known phenomena of our time: obsessions, aggressions, addictions, fringe groups, "activist" movements of every description all bear its stamp. To a consciousness that meets it with affirmation it appears in positive form in archetypal images, as artistic or scientific inspiration, or as a compensatory impulse driving towards individuation. Four hundred years ago it inducted the alchemists into the strange mysteries of their opus and their pseudo-chemical nature mysticism. It has undergone a secret renaissance in the art of our century. Art has become its tool and art as "mysticism" its prophet, the exponent of an irrational spirit, of an immemorial archetypal numen which, reactivated, has burst forth out of the unconscious by way of compensation into the age of modern Christian culture and technological achievement.

In the course of the years modern art outgrew the revolutionary mystique of its beginnings and became the style of the epoch. Nowadays but few people know what it was all about when artists had to "break the mirror of life so that we may look being in the face" (Franz Marc), and shape the reality behind the flux of appearances. Even among artists themselves this knowledge has begun to fade. The spiritual and mystical goal of art has ceased to be important. Non-objective representation, a major trend of modern art, endless variations on the transformation of the concrete world into transpersonal symbolisms, or into irreality, absurdity or hideousness have now become aesthetic convention.

The satisfaction the observer feels when contemplating a modern work of art is explained psychologically—leaving aside the conscious motivations of taste, connoisseurship, etc.—by the spirit informing it, which demands to be recognised as a content of the collective unconscious and assimilated into consciousness. Being an expression of the constellated unconscious, modern art involves the observer personally; it makes a direct impact, and for this reason "understanding" does not necessarily presuppose an intellectual or aesthetic grasp of the art work but can just as well be unconscious and intuitive. Even disgust, because of the violent emotion that often accompanies it, is proof that the artist has hit the inner mark.

In his once popular books *Abstraction and Empathy* (1907) and *Formprobleme der Gotik* (1912), Wilhelm Worringer explained that abstraction in art was an expression of man's metaphysical fear. It is a symptom of man's turning away from the confusing chaos of the world, a flight from life due to a profound disquiet.

Expanding on Worringer's thesis, Jung, in his *Psychological Types*,[40] compares abstraction in art with the turning away from the agitations of the outer world that is characteristic of the introvert, while objective art would correspond rather to the extraverted attitude, which accepts the objective world and apprehends it through empathy, sometimes at the cost of introspection. Such a type-correlation should not lead one to suppose that the abstract artist can be classed from the start as an introvert. This may or not be the case. But at all events the tendency to abstraction can be taken as a symptom of a collective introversive movement originating in the unconscious, a turning to the inner world. It may be regarded as compensating the conscious attitude of extreme extraversion which is so widespread today. Abstract art would then be the collective expression of the lack of introversion in the individual. One could, however, put the argument the other way round and for once seek the compensatory tendency in the *conscious* attitude. On this premise the extraverted bustle of modern life and the hectic struggle for still more sophisticated and quicker ways of conquering the outer world would serve the purpose of compensating or shouting down a secret, increasingly pervasive fear. Fear is an essential element in the psyche of modern man. It lurks in the unconscious and is one of mainsprings of modern art.

The early masters of modern art were aware that their abstractions, their turning away from outer reality, from nature and man were a consequence of suffering and fear. During the First World War, early in 1915, Klee wrote in his *Diary*: "The more horrifying this world becomes (as it is in these days) the more art becomes abstract; while a world at peace produces realistic art." To Franz Marc, abstraction offered a refuge from the evil and ugliness in this world. "Very early in life I felt that man was ugly. The animals seemed to me more lovely and pure, yet even among them I discovered so much that was revolting and hideous that my painting, from inner necessity, instinctively became more and more schematic and abstract."

But very early it also turned out that the retreat from the outer world, from the "locus of anxiety", recoiled upon the artist's vision of the inner world. The "other side" was far from offering a harmonious refuge from the torments of life, and the spirit of nature was anything but a bringer of peace. All too many contemporary works of art bear the signature of anxiety, despair and aggressiveness, of agony, discord, contempt and callousness. They reflect, as in a mirror, the suffering and dereliction of man in external reality. The terrors of the outer world, from which art had fled, are revealed as the agonies of the inner world.

In abstract works of art the realms of consciousness and of the diurnal world retire into the background.[41] The frequently heard objection that the act of painting as such requires the co-operation of consciousness even from the non-objective artist is not tenable. The products of "action painting", initiated by Jackson Pollock and executed in a trancelike state, often attain a strange intensity of expression and show that at times even the most tenuous formal relation to consciousness can be ignored by the modern artist.

From the psychological standpoint, creative art is in most cases a collaboration between inspiration and the formative impulse. Yet, as Jung says: "One person will stress the *forms* into which he can work this material, and will therefore believe that he is the creator of what he finds within himself. Another will lay most weight on what is observed; he will therefore speak of it as a phenomenon, while remaining conscious of his own receptive attitude. The truth probably lies between the two: true expression consists in giving form to what is observed."[42] In the case of great artists the two standpoints often alternate or work together. When Picasso says: "*Je ne cherche pas, je trouve,*" he is speaking of inspiration. Bur when he repeats a motif in countless variations or tirelessly reworks the same painting over and over again, then the conscious, formative impulse is at work.

The turning away of modern art from the realism of the outer world—"breaking the mirror of life"—must be understood as the artist's fascination with the inner reality, as the challenge put to him by the topical question of an invisible background of life that cannot be rationally comprehended. His inturned gaze opened up a grandiose vision of the "undefined and indefinable", and modern art, whether nonobjective or representational, became the exponent of an unconscious spirit, or a symbol of the irrational that compensates our rationality. What from the psychological standpoint may appear to be a one-sided view of the world is actually the uncompromising drive of the artistic will.

A psychological approach to modern art and its confrontation with the unconscious has, let it be expressly emphasised, nothing to do with judging it, or with setting a higher value on one art movement than on another. Aesthetic content, style and taste are of as little concern to the psychologist as competence or incompetence, mastery, genius or decadent imitation. But the intimation of an invisible, existential reality behind the world of objects is a general problem of our time, and that is why it concerns psychology. "Modern art" must be understood as a specific expression of our epoch. It can be described as an attempt to enrich the representation of the ephemeral world by the infusion of a changeless reality independent of time and space. In its way, Jung's work is a similar answer to the contemporary situation. It, too, is an attempt to add a new, deeper dimension to our understanding of the world, though for Jung objective reality never lost its fundamental importance.

### Inner Experience through Mescalin and LSD
Due regard for consciousness as well as the unconscious, recognition of outer as well as inner reality, were for Jung the

indispensable foundations of a life meaningfully lived. He knew, however, how difficult it is to follow the "middle way". "In my picture of the world there is a vast outer realm and an equally vast inner realm; between these two stands man, facing now one and now the other, and, according to temperament and disposition, taking the one for the absolute truth by denying or sacrificing the other."[43]

One-sidedness never doubts itself. It deems itself superior, and is a temptation although the certitudes it offers have always proved deceptive. Unremarked, the counter-reality exists and the psychic counter-forces live on. Overlooked or denied by the conscious mind, they exert their influence in the form of unconscious tendencies and impulses. This is as true of the psychology of the individual as of the currents of contemporary history. Neither technology nor the dominance of reason can stem the tide of unconscious, irrational counter-forces which reduce the certitudes of the rational mind to absurdity. The irrational has infiltrated science, art and literature, it is already a co-determining factor in our picture of the world this century, which still proudly styles itself the "age of enlightenment" or the "technological age". There are also irrational currents secretly at work beyond the confines of the generally accepted world picture. As "mantic arts" —astrology, chiromancy, geomancy, magic, etc. —they have penetrated into every social sphere and play a far greater role than one would like to admit. In extreme, though by no means rare, cases they have become unavowed substitutes for religion.

The more confidently and clamorously the rational aims of life are stressed, the more intensely the irrational, or the longing for the irrational, makes itself felt as an unconscious compensation. The need for a balance of this kind also lies at the root of the widespread interest in the inner perceptions and experiences produced by mescalin, lysergic acid (LSD), and

similar drugs. Arguments for and against are bandied about by
scientists and flit through the pages of newspapers and
illustrated magazines. An ever-increasing number of people,
above all the young, as much from inner emptiness as from
unsatisfied spiritual curiosity, seek refuge in the phantas-
magoria of the pill. By weakening consciousness the drug un-
locks the door to the world of the unconscious and, because of
the latter's numinosity, can lead to religious or pseudo-
religious experiences. Aldous Huxley described his experience
with mescalin as a "sacramental vision of reality".[44]

Under the influence of mescalin, LSD and related chemicals
there is a lowering of the threshold of consciousness but, as in
waking fantasies, the perceiving, experiencing and discriminating function of the ego is preserved, or is said to be
preserved. They produce a condition of psychic dissociation
not unlike a psychosis; indeed, the condition has been termed
"model psychosis".

Huxley reports that as a result of his mescalin experience his
whole conception of consciousness changed: the belief that our
"reduced awareness" is the only possible means of apprehending the world no longer held. In the intoxication of mescalin
he found himself confronted with "Mind at Large", where
"everything shone with the Inner Light, and was infinite in
its significance".[45] He had the impression that in this all-
embracing awareness he could see "the divine source of all
existence".[46] Huxley took the mescalin intoxication to be the
revelation of a metaphysical reality. From the psychological
point of view it was an experience of the numinosity of the
unconscious, condensed in the archetypal image of an "inner
light" shining at the heart of things, and in the hitherto
undreamt-of significance of the objects around him: the bamboo
legs of a chair, the folds in his trousers, a vase of flowers. He
saw the flowers "shining with their own inner light and all but

quivering under the pressure of the significance with which they were charged".[47] The "pure Being" of things had become a projection carrier for the numinous reality of the unconscious.

In his second book on mescalin experiences, *Heaven and Hell*, Huxley expanded on his report: the experiences produced by the drug can be as terrifying as they are glorious. The revelation of heaven or paradise with its blazing colours and infinite significance is followed by that of a hell with Dantesque torments. Huxley thus provided· experimental confirmation of Jung's statement that the paradoxical nature of the archetype reveals itself to consciousness in antithetical images.

Mescalin is an alkaloid of the Mexican cactus which the Indians call peyotl. In the Indian folk-religions of Mexico the consumption of peyotl, or of "sacred mushrooms" containing a similar toxin, occupies a central place in their religious ceremonies. According to Karl Kerényi, an intoxicating drink was consumed by the celebrants at Eleusis. During the initiation it appears to have evoked the "epopteia", the supreme vision of the goddess Demeter.[48]

We know today that in certain cases the dissociation of consciousness produced by LSD is irreversible, that criminal impulses may be released or a depression set in, not infrequently leading to suicide. On the other hand, it is being used in modern psychotherapy. As it induces in the patient an immediate and intense contact with the unconscious, quicker cures were hoped for than by the classical analyses which usually last a very long time. In a somewhat sensationally got-up report on a successful LSD analysis conducted under medical supervision, *My Self and I*: Constance Newland writes: "Techniques such as dream interpretations or free associations or slips of the tongue might be likened to the routes taken by a covered wagon, trekking its way across a continent to reach

the ocean of the unconscious: LSD offers a non-stop jet
flight."[49] Although high velocities and time-saving procedures are attractive considerations nowadays, doctors are
still not clear about the value or non-value of LSD and
mescalin in psychotherapy. The negative psychic side-effects
of the drugs have understandably given rise to misdoubts.

Jung evinced great interest in scientific experiments with
mescalin. He found in them confirmation of his researches on
the manifestations of the unconscious and its numinosity. He
rejected the use of drugs in psychotherapy or as a means to
spiritual experience and a religious re-attunement of man, as
could hardly be otherwise considering his reverence for nature
and its specific rhythms and laws. An artificially induced
experience of the unconscious does not as a rule accord with the
development and maturity of the personality. This discrepancy
harbours a danger, because any content that emerges from the
unconscious into consciousness involves a spiritual or moral
task which, if not accomplished, leads to misunderstandings,
complications, suffering and illness. Without the corresponding
spiritual work of assimilating and integrating the contents
evoked by the drug, the experience, however fascinating, loses
its value and its meaning.

Though there is little mention of mescalin in Jung's work,[50]
he was constantly being asked what he thought about it. It is of
interest that a Catholic priest wrote to him about LSD only
two years after its synthesis by Hoffman. Jung replied (April
1954):[51]

"Is the LSD drug mescalin? It has indeed very curious
effects—*vide* Aldous Huxley!—of which I know far too little.
I don't know either what its psychotherapeutic value with
neurotic or psychotic patients is. I only know there is no point
in wishing to know more of the collective unconscious than

one gets through dreams and intuition. The more you know of it, the greater and heavier becomes your moral burden, because unconscious contents are transformed into your individual tasks and duties as soon as they begin to become conscious. Do you want to increase loneliness and misunderstanding? Do you want to find more and more complications and increasing responsibilities? You get enough of it. If I once could say that I have done everything I know I had to do, then perhaps I should realise a legitimate need to take mescalin. But if I should take it now, I would not be sure at all that I had not taken it out of idle curiosity. I should hate the thought that I had touched on the sphere where the paint is made that colours the world, where the light is created that makes shine the splendour of the dawn, the lines and shapes of all form, the sound that fills the orbit, the thought that illuminates the darkness of the void. There are some poor impoverished creatures perhaps, for whom mescalin would be a heaven-sent gift without a counter-poison, but I am profoundly mistrustful of the 'pure gifts of the Gods'. You pay dearly for them. *Quidquid id est timeo Danaos et dona ferentes.*

"This is not the point at all, to know of or about the unconscious, nor does the story end here; on the contrary it is how and where you begin the real quest. If you are too unconscious it is a great relief to know a bit of the collective unconscious. But it soon becomes dangerous to know more, because one does not learn at the same time how to balance it through a conscious equivalent. This is the mistake Aldous Huxley makes. (It is really the mistake of our age. We think it is enough to discover new things, but we don't realise that knowing more demands a corresponding development of morality. Radioactive clouds over Japan, Calcutta and Saskatchewan point to a progressive poisoning of the universal atmosphere.) He does not know that he is in the role of the *Zauberlehrling* [52] who has learned from his master how to call the ghosts, but did not know how to get rid of them again . . ."

The drug is and remains an all too convenient substitute for human effort and spontaneous experience. Like Jung, Thomas Mann condemns Huxley's recommendation of mescalin and warns against the unpredictable consequences of its use. He calls Huxley's book *The Doors of Perception* an example of "escapism" and mescalin experience "unprincipled aesthetic self-gratification".[53]

The misgivings expressed by Jung and Thomas Mann are certainly justified when one considers the misuse of these drugs by immature, labile persons craving for new sensations. Yet it should not be overlooked that LSD and its affiliates are an important tool in the hands of responsible psychological researchers. They have an immense value for the further investigation of the unconscious and its phenomena; they facilitate for the so-called normal, ordinary man a progressively deeper descent into the unconscious and are therefore a sort of chemical key that might carry the exploration of the unconscious to levels completely unknown at present.

The drugs are not only a scientific tool, they also open new —or age-old—ways to a type of experience which, for want of a better word, those who have known it are impelled to describe as "religious" or "mystical". A 52-year-old engineer, apparently a quite simple man with no religious inclinations, gives the following account of his experience with LSD:

"Although consciousness of self seemed extinguished, I knew that the boundaries of my being had been dissolved and that all other boundaries were also dissolved. All, including what had been myself, was an ever more rapid molecular whirling that then became something else, a pure and seething energy that was the whole of being. This energy, neither hot nor cold, was experienced as a white and radiant fire . . . The flux of Being streamed inexorably, unswervingly towards the One.

"At what I can only call the 'core' of this flux was God, and I cannot explain how it was that I, who seemed to have no identity at all, yet experienced myself as filled with God, and then as (whatever this may mean), *passing through* God and into a Oneness wherein it seemed God, Being, and a mysterious unnameable One constituted together what I can only designate the All. What 'I' experienced in this All so far transcends my powers of description that to speak, as I must, of an ineffably rapturous Sweetness is an approximation not less feeble than if I were to describe a candle and hope to capture with my words all the blazing glory of the sun."[54]

Here we have a genuine experience of the numinous such as Jung was also concerned with. One dare not dismiss out of hand any instrument that makes a *unio mystica* of this kind possible. It goes without saying, however, that from the psycho-therapeutic standpoint in particular, and also that of individuation, the man who is conscious of his responsibilities cannot stop at ecstatic visionary experiences but must complete and deepen them through sober reflection and assimilate their meaning into his life. In this way the danger of losing contact with his own reality and with his environment is neutralised or at least reduced to a minimum, and also the danger of hankering for repetitions of the experience for its own sake.

# 6

## INDIVIDUATION

### Active Imagination and Life

The natural way to personal experience of the collective unconscious is opened by dreams and, less commonly, by visions, hallucinations, synchronistic phenomena, etc. Besides these spontaneous manifestations Jung, as mentioned already, introduced into analytical practice another method of voluntarily making contact with the deeper layers of the unconscious. It is a kind of introspection or meditation, based on fantasy activity, which he called *active imagination*.[1] The first reaction to the proposal that one should "imagine actively" usually consists in suspicion and resistance, which appears understandable enough in view of the obvious irrationality of such a procedure. But for Jung the whole point of it lay precisely in the purposelessness of unrestrained fantasy activity, in the element of play that has to be taken very much in earnest, and he cites Schiller: "The creative activity of imagination frees man from his bondage to the 'nothing but' and raises him to the status of one who plays. As Schiller says, man is completely human only when he is at play."[2]

The frequent objection that the alleged "fantasies" are consciously thought out, that the images therefore do not come from the unconscious at all, is unfounded. Admittedly there is "wishful thinking", which is not a product of the unconscious but is arranged by the ego. Wishful thinking is manipulated fantasy, and its inauthentic nature is easily discernible from the absence of archetypal motifs and numinous images. Moreover the element of surprise is lacking, as well as anything that might be felt to be distressing or frightening.[3] Genuine imagination is inspired by the unconscious; the ego confronts the images as though they were reality, not only perceiving them passively, but actively participating in their play and reaching an understanding with them. The images are self-manifestations of the psyche and may therefore be taken as fragments of those waking dreams dreamt below the threshold of consciousness, but which it does not perceive because of its preoccupation with processes in the external world. The aim of active imagination is to find a middle position between conscious and unconscious, having "a quality of conjoined opposites". Jung also spoke of a "transcendent function of opposites".[4] A precondition for the success of active imagination is that it shall not be a pretext for flight from life. "Fantasies are no substitute for living; they are the fruits of the spirit which fall to him who pays his tribute to life. The shirker experiences nothing but his own morbid fear, and it yields him no meaning."[5]

It is not possible to decide with certainty whether consciousness predominates over the unconscious in active imagination, or the unconscious over consciousness. This is why Jung gave now one and now the other the leading role. "In coming to terms with the unconscious . . . the ego takes the lead, but the unconscious must be allowed to have its say too — *audiatur et altera pars*."[6] Against this early formulation we must set a later one: "A dark impulse is the ultimate arbiter of the pattern, an unconscious *a priori* precipitates itself into plastic form . . . Over the whole procedure there seems to reign a dim foreknowledge not only of the pattern but of its meaning."[7] In the end it is an interplay of conscious and unconscious, the leader often becoming the led and vice versa.

Although Jung and his patients used the method of active
imagination for many years, it was a long time before he was
able to discern a law and a meaning in the variety of complicated patterns and configurations they produced, whether "in
the form of dancing, painting, drawing, or modelling". Only
gradually did he discover that "I was witnessing the spontaneous
manifestation of an unconscious process which was merely
assisted by the technical ability of the patient, and to which I
later gave the name 'individuation process'."[8] In active imagination the process, as in dreams and other manifestations of the
unconscious, portrays itself in a succession of images, so that at
least in part it can be perceived by the conscious mind. In
referring to "an unconscious *a priori*", "a dim foreknowledge"
that reigns over the whole procedure, Jung is alluding to the
archetype of the self, which is the driving force behind the
formation of images and arranges the unconscious happenings.
Thanks to it, the fantasy does not normally go off the rails but
in a surprising way always arrives at its destination, although
the fantasist may have the feeling of being "utterly exposed to
the boundless subjective vagaries of chance".[9]

As may be deduced from the passages we have quoted,
individuation does not consist solely of successions of images
from the unconscious. These are only part of the process, representing its inner or spiritual reality. Its necessary complement
is outer reality, the development of individuality and its
attendant fate. Both aspects of the process are regulated by the
powerful archetype of the self. In other words, in the course of
individuation the self emerges into the world of consciousness,
while at the same time its originally psychoid nature splits
apart, so that it manifests itself as much in inner images as in
the events of real life. Hence Jung expanded his definition of
the individuation process as a succession of inner images by
describing it as "life" itself: "In the last analysis every life is

the realisation of a whole, that is, of a self, for which reason this realisation can also be called 'individuation'."[10] Basically, individuation consists of constantly renewed, constantly needed attempts to amalgamate the inner images with outer experience. Or to put it differently, it is the endeavour to "make what fate intends to do with us entirely our own intention" (W. Bergengruen). In successful moments a part of the self is actualised as a union of inside and outside. Then a man can repose in himself, because self-fulfilled, and an aura of authenticity emanates from him.

The meaning of life, for Jung, is the realisation of the self. "All life is bound to individual carriers who realise it . . . But every carrier is charged with an individual destiny and destination [the self], and the realisation of these alone makes sense of life."[11] The significance of this sober statement only dawns on us when we consider that the archetype of the self is "nameless, ineffable",[12] a hidden X whose concretisations are indistinguishable from God-images. Accordingly, the individuation process culminates not in the fullest possible life lived for its own sake, and not in profounder intellectual understanding: its meaning flows from the numinosity of the self. To put it in religious language, individuation has to be understood as the realisation of the "divine" in man.

The formulation of the meaning of life in these terms is certainly not intended either as a dogma or as an article of faith. It stems, as Jung repeatedly emphasised, only from the interpretation of psychic phenomena, and every interpretation is subjective. The critical intellect is, of course, confronted again and again by the question of the objective validity of facts and experiences that can be verified psychologically. Yet "it is difficult to see how this question could be answered, as the intellect lacks the necessary criteria. Anything that might

F

serve as a criterion is subject in turn to the critical question of
validity. The only thing that can decide here is the preponder-
ance of psychic facts".[13] Faced with this uncertainty, Jung did
not rule out a reversal of his own as of every other interpretation
of meaning: "True, 'sense' is often something that could just
as well be called 'nonsense', for there is no little incom-
mensurability between the mystery of existence and human understanding. 'Sense' and 'nonsense' are merely man-made labels
which serve to give us a reasonably valid sense of direction."[14]

Scientific research ends by establishing that the archetype of
the self reaches its goal in every life. In a "natural individuation" it does so even if the world of the unconscious remains in
darkness and not a single archetypal image is seen, let alone
understood in all its implications.[15] An experience of meaning
comes—aside from living faith—only from a deepening of
external reality through recognition of its numinous background.
"Life that just happens in and for itself is not real life: it is
real only when it is known",[16] "real life" being understood
here as "meaningful life". By becoming conscious of its transpersonal connections and images, and experiencing their
numinosity, we get an inkling of powers which operate autonomously behind our being and doing, creating an order in our
lives, as well as behind the seeming fortuitousness of events.
We then experience, or intuit, how vast is the nexus of life
and the goal towards which it is striving, no matter whether
this be interpreted as sense or nonsense, and no matter whether
any such interpretation is sought or not. Jung did seek an
interpretation, trying to "create" meaning although fully aware
of the limitations of every interpretation. As a doctor he was
faced again and again with the need to interpret meaning:
"Man can live the most amazing things if they make sense to
him. But the difficulty is to create that sense."[17]

Even if we are fully cognisant of the limits imposed by the theory of knowledge, the "indwelling" and unfolding of the numinous archetype of the self in man is an experience that may have grave consequences. The danger of confusing individuation with becoming a god-man or a superman is painfully evident. The tragic or grotesque consequences of such a misunderstanding can be avoided only if the ego-personality can bear coming to terms with the self without losing sight of the reality of our human limitations and our ordinariness. "The self in its divinity (i.e., the archetype) . . . can become conscious only within our consciousness. And it can do that only if the ego stands firm. The self must become as small as, and yet smaller than, the ego, although it is the ocean of divinity: 'God is as small as me;, says Angelus Silesius. It must become the 'thumbling in the heart'," Jung wrote in a letter (September 1943) explaining the paradox of realising the self.[18] The self is the immeasurable expanse of the psyche and at the same time its innermost core. The "thumbling in the heart" is an allusion of the childlike nature of divinity.[19] It is the Indian *purusha*, "smaller than small, greater than great".[20] Christ, too, is venerated both as the ruler of the world and a child.

The individuation process requires a ruthlessly honest confrontation with the contents of the unconscious, and this is sufficient to damp down any fits of ebullience. It holds many darknesses and painful insights in store which are conducive to modesty. Anyone who nevertheless looks with disdain upon the "unenlightened" or preaches "truths" has become the victim of his own dottiness. He has identified his ego with the contents of the unconscious. The psychological term for this is inflation. It ranges from more or less harmless pomposity to the complete extinction of the ego in the image constellated by the unconscious. Jung gives as an example of an inflation ending in psychosis the story of a sentimental youth who had fallen in love with a girl. When he discovered that the girl would have nothing to do with him, "he was so desperate that he went straight to the river to drown himself. It was late at night, and the stars gleamed up at him from the dark water. It seemed to him that the stars were swimming two by two down the river, and a wonderful feeling came over him. He forgot his suicidal intentions and gazed fascinated at the strange, sweet drama. And gradually he became aware that every star was a face, and that all these pairs were lovers, who were carried along locked in a dreaming embrace. An entirely new understanding came to him: all had changed—his fate, his disappointment, even his love, receded and fell away. The memory of the girl grew distant, blurred; but instead, he felt with complete certainty that untold riches were promised him. He knew that an immense treasure lay hidden for him in the neighbouring observatory. The result was that he was arrested by the police at four o'clock in the morning, attempting to break into the observatory.

"What had happened? His poor head had glimpsed a Dantesque vision, whose loveliness he could never have grasped had he read it in a poem. But he saw it, and it transformed him. What had hurt him most was now far away; a new and undreamed-of world of stars, tracing their silent courses far beyond this grievous earth, had opened out to him the moment he crossed 'Proserpine's threshold'. The intuition of untold wealth—and who could fail to be touched by this thought?—came to him like a revelation. For his poor turnip-head it was too much. He did not drown in the river, but in an eternal image, and its beauty perished with him."[21]

Individuation pursues its course in a meaningful way only in our everyday existence. Acceptance of life as it is, of its banality, its extraordinariness, respect for the body and its demands, are

just as much a prerequisite for individuation as a relationship
to one's fellow men. The more insistent the spiritual quality
of the self becomes, the more our consciousness is expanded
through the integration of psychic contents, the deeper we must
strike our roots in reality, in our own earth, the body, and the
more responsibly we must be bound to our nearest and dearest
and to the environment,[22] because the "worldly" side of the
archetype and its instinctual qualities must be realised too.
Individuation can thus go in two typical but opposite directions. If the spiritual aspect of wholeness is unconscious and
therefore undifferentiated, the goal is to expand consciousness
through deeper insight into the laws that hold the psyche
together. It is a question of sacrificing the primitive, un-
reflecting man in ourselves. If, on the other hand, our consciousness has become alienated from the instincts, then the
worldly aspect of wholeness is constellated, and it is a matter
of accepting reality and working on it, of re-establishing a
connection with nature and our fellows. In the case of modern
man this oftenrequires the sacrifice of a one-sided intellectualism.

Both directions correspond to archetypal situations at all
levels of culture, for which reason they appear as constantly
recurring variants in the symbolism of myths and fairy-tales.
Sometimes it is the task of the hero to conquer an animal or
dragon (instinct) in order to gain the treasure (the self). And
sometimes it is his task to protect and nourish the beast at the
risk of his own life, whereupon it will help him in his quest
for the treasure.

The goal of individuation, the realisation of the self, is never
fully attained. Because it transcends consciousness, the archetype of the self can never be wholly apprehended, and because
of its boundlessness never completely lived in actual life.
"Successful individuation" is never total, it is only an optimal

achievement of wholeness. "But it is just the impossibility of this task that makes it so significant," Jung once wrote in this connection. "A task that is possible, i.e., soluble, never appeals to our superiority." That is what individuation does, because we are not equal to it. "It appeals to our superiority, and perhaps that is just what is needed. There may be tasks we can solve better with inferiority than with superiority. As long as my superiority is not in absolute jeopardy, a bit of me remains untouched by life."[23] Jung reverts to his theme in "The Psychology of the Transference": "The goal [of individuation] is important only as an idea. The essential thing is the *opus* which leads to the goal: *that* is the goal of a lifetime."[24] Because of the self's drive towards realisation, life appears as a task of the highest order, and therein lies the possibility of interpreting its meaning, which does not exclude the possibility of defeat.

The integration of the self is, like all life, bound, as we have said, to individual carriers, and "every carrier is charged with an individual destiny and destination".[25] The unknowable and timeless archetype of the self assumes a specific and unique form in everyone, and the task, the goal of individuation lies in fulfilling one's own destiny and vocation. "Vocation acts like a law of God from which there is no escape."[26] In reality it is an aspect of the self, that paradoxical totality which is at once eternal and unique.

The "eternal" aspect of the self is concretised in the imagery of the unconscious by impersonal symbols—geometrical or stereometric figures (triangle, square, circle, cube, sphere, etc.), by numbers or groups of numbers, by light and cosmic phenomena, sacred objects, or else by abstractions (the "unknowable"). The "unique" individual aspect is represented rather by sublime, even divine, figures of the same sex with quite definite features, more rarely by an inner voice. It goes without saying that this is not an unvarying rule, and that there are overlappings or combinations of one group and the other.

Jung used the terms "self" and "wholeness" both for the irrepresentable, transcendental archetype and for the "entelechy" of the individual. Besides the formulation "self" as a collective, boundless and ungraspable entity we also find "his self" or "her self" in the sense of that individual's specific peculiarity; and besides the indefinite or general term "wholeness" the specific "wholeness of the dreamer", etc., just as in ordinary speech "man" means not only an individual man but the totality of the species.

The sometimes confusing use of "self" in this twofold sense is occasioned psychologically by its function of uniting opposites. In *Aion* Jung compares the archetype of wholeness with the dogmatic figure of Christ, who as "an historical personage is unitemporal and unique; as God, universal and eternal".[27] The same is true in the psychological realm: "The self as the essence of individuality is unitemporal and unique; as an archetypal symbol it is a God-image and therefore universal and eternal."[28] For this reason the concepts "destiny and destination", or "entelechy", and "self" fuse together: the one is contained in the other.

Consciousness experiences the self in both its aspects: as a universal and eternal symbol and as "the completest expression of that fateful combination we call individuality".[29] But even this "incomparable uniqueness"[30] can never be fully attained, it remains the task and the goal of individuation.

### Historical Order and Eternal Order

While the distinction between the individual and the universal nature of the self is not carried through consistently in Jung's work and perhaps cannot be, he does distinguish rigorously between the ego-personality and the transpersonal self. They are the great antagonists in the drama of individuation.

Jung tells us in his memoirs how he gradually became conscious of the antithetical nature of ego and self. In order to differentiate between them, he called his ego, with all its limitations as citizen, doctor and paterfamilias, "Personality No. 1", whereas "Personality No. 2" stood for a timeless factor influencing him from a transpersonal world, which even as a child he had experienced as a "superior personality", an "old man of great authority" who appeared to him in various guises, and also as an inner voice. "No. 1" and "No. 2" are modest enough appellations considering their content, yet Jung could legitimately claim to have already described these two factors or figures in his scientific work. Also, he was chary of portentous words; where he himself was concerned, the bare numbers were sufficient.

This naturally gave rise to misunderstandings. Knowledge of the inner world and the existence of a consciousness-transcending self or "superior personality" have nowadays all but passed into oblivion, and we stand helpless and bewildered before any psychic experience of a timeless background of being. The objective world, anything measurable, fascinates and enslaves us, while the irrational, the inner-directed, the transcendental remains unnoticed or is denied. Life no longer points beyond itself. And yet the assertion that man partakes of two realities —the conscious and unconscious, ego and self, history and eternity, the personal and transpersonal, the sacred and profane, existence and essence—is evidence of an inner knowledge which has risen up again and again in the course of human history, and again passed away. Most religions, Christianity included, address themselves to the inner, spiritual, immortal man whose kingdom is "not of this world" and yet becomes a reality in this world.

The interweaving of the conscious and unconscious, profane and sacred reality is an integral part of the experience of human wholeness, and it is for this reason that the connections between psychology and religion became for Jung the starting-point for his "creation" of meaning. They will be discussed in greater detail later.[31] In its recognition of archetypal dual nature of man, Jung's psychology joins hands with Paul Tillich's theology. Tillich, too, assigns man to two different orders of being: a historical order, which is primarily the "order of growth and death", and another that is "the Word of God" and eternal. Man "transcends everything pertaining to the historical order, all the heights and depths of his existence. Unlike all other beings, he transgresses the bounds of his given world. He participates in something infinite, in an order that is not ephemeral."[32] The two orders of being, the historical and the divine, belong together. "Though they can never be identical, they are interwoven."[33] The eternal order is manifest in the historical order, which amounts psychologically to saying that the self is unfolded in the world of consciousness.

Man transcends himself, Tillich goes on, by entering into a timeless order he feels is divine; in psychological terms, he is anchored in the unconscious and penetrates with his consciousness ever deeper into this hidden realm of the numinous. On its side, the divine order unfolds in the reverse direction. Though it is eternal, infinite, inapprehensible, it pours as the "Word of God" out of transcendental reality into the restricted, history-bound life of man. Correspondingly, the unconscious is funnelled into consciousness and is experienced in the form of numinous archetypal contents and figures, moreover the transcendental archetype of the self is realised in man and his life. Conscious and unconscious, ego and self, stand in the same reciprocal and dynamic relationship as Tillich's two orders of being: they interpenetrate but are not identical.

An experience of the dual nature of man is not unknown to thoughtful people today. Hermann Hesse, Eugene O'Neill, Julian Green and others, not to speak of the surrealists, show man leading a strange double life on the borderland between the earthly and the divine, the temporal and eternal, nature and dream. In the memoirs of his childhood, Sartre too gives an account of his dual nature; but, in keeping with his philosophy, he remains stuck in the profane world. Once he interrupts the story of his fantasies about his own greatness and importance as a famous writer with the following reflection: "Faith, even when profound, is never complete. It has to be endlessly maintained or, at least, preserved from destruction. I was dedicated and famous, I *had* my tomb in the Père-Lachaise cemetery and perhaps in the Panthéon. I had my avenue in Paris and my side-streets and squares in the provinces and abroad: yet, in the very heart of my optimism, I retained an invisible and nameless suspicion of my lack of substance. In the Sainte-Anne's asylum a sick man shouted from his bed: 'I am the Prince! Put the Grand Duke under arrest.' Someone went up to him and whispered: 'Wipe your nose,' and he wiped it. He was asked: 'What's your trade?' and he replied softly: 'A shoemaker,' and started shouting again. We are all like that man, I imagine; certainly I was like him when I entered my ninth year: I was both prince and shoemaker."[34]

But, so far as our feeling for life and the experience of meaning are concerned, it makes a tremendous difference whether man's dual nature, as with Sartre, is transposed to the social plane and secularised, or whether it spans the immeasurable distance between the polarities divinity and humanity, eternity and history, dream and reality.

*Freedom and Bondage*
The individuation process is a progressive realisation of whole-

ness in life and it takes the form of a confrontation between conscious and unconscious, ego and self. In this confrontation the ego appears at first to be the loser. Originally sprung from the self, "the ego stands to the self as the moved to the mover, or as object to subject, because the determining factors which radiate out from the self surround the ego on all sides and are therefore supraordinate to it".[35] On one occasion Jung actually speaks of the "passion of the ego",[36] for in individuation it is the fate of the ego-personality to be absorbed into the greater circle of the self and to be robbed of its illusion of freedom. The ego and, by extension, the individual, "suffers, so to speak, from the violence done to him by the self".[37] Hence individuation is always "as much of a fatality as a fulfillment".[38]

Considering the ascendency of the self, individuation can be regarded only as a deterministic process: a "dim foreknowledge" seems to reign over it. Yet that is only one side of the picture, for the ego insists on its role as the centre of consciousness.[39] In spite of its manifest dependence on the self, it retains an inalienable sense of freedom which is the precondition of human dignity and the necessary basis of moral responsibility. Above all, the ego is the vehicle of all experience: without it, individuation could not become a reality, for we would not be aware of anything or anybody to individuate *on*. In this sense, the self is in a position of relative dependence on the ego: the ego creates it, as it were, by the conscious realisation and actualisation of unconscious contents. It discerns the images of the self in dreams and its patternings in life, and, through this observation and acceptance of the observed, it lifts the self out of the darkness of the unconscious into the light of consciousness.

Sooner or later, genuine individuation requires of the individuant a willingness to give up the claims of his ego-personality in favour of the self as a supraordinate authority, and to renounce them without forfeiting himself. Individuation always involves sacrifice, a "passion of the ego". But "it does not mean just letting yourself be passively taken: it is a conscious and deliberate self-surrender, which proves that you have full control of yourself, that is, of your ego".[40] Nevertheless, you are driven to this free or voluntary self-surrender by the self, by its striving for development and actualisation. The "more compendious personality . . . takes the ego into its service";[41] the ego becomes the representative and executor of the self in the world of consciousness.

The reciprocal relation between ego and self, or man and self, underlies the paradoxical saying of the alchemists that the philosophical stone—a symbol of the self—is both "son" and "father". "Up to a point we create the self by making ourselves conscious of our unconscious contents, and to that extent it is our son. That is why the alchemists called their incorruptible substance—which means precisely the self—the *filius philosophorum*. But we are forced to make this effort by the unconscious presence of the self, which is all the time urging us to overcome our unconsciousness. From that point of view the self is the father."[42] To express it in another image: man's wholeness, originally hidden and "imprisoned" in the unconscious, proves in the course of individuation to be the actual prison, albeit a "compendious" one. This discovery of their captivity will horrify small-minded people, but "the man who is inwardly great will know that the long expected friend of his soul, the immortal one, has now really come, 'to lead captivity captive' (Ephesians 4:8)."[43]

The relation between ego and self and their mutual dependence confront the psychology of individuation with the perennial question of freedom. Without freedom, individuation would be a senseless mechanism, worth neither thought nor effort. It would be, in Jung's words, "fatality" not "fulfilment". Conversely, it would lose all meaning if there were complete freedom, for it could then go just as well in one direction as in the other. No decision would be needed, no criterion, no goal.

As with all questions bordering on the transcendental, the only answer psychology can give is an antinomian one: man is free and is not free.[44] He is not free to choose his destiny, but his consciousness makes him free to accept it as a task laid upon him by nature.[45] If he takes the responsibility for individuation he voluntarily submits to the self—in religious language, he submits to the will of God. Yet submission does not do away with the sense of freedom. On the contrary, only by sacrificing it does he justify his freedom and validate his responsibility for his actions and decisions. Sacrifice is an affirmation of the task life sets him. It carries man beyond himself and can thus lead to an authentic experience of meaning. A few months before his tragic death (18 September 1961) Dag Hammarskjöld wrote in his Diary: "I don't know Who — or What—put the question, I don't know when it was put. I don't even remember answering. But at some moment I did answer *Yes* to Someone—or Something—and from that hour I was certain that existence is meaningful and that, therefore, my life, in self-surrender, had a goal."[46]

Man is free to expand his consciousness. Unlike animals and plants, he is not only part of nature but is created as a being endowed with spirit. Only man asks about God. Unique in creation, he has in large measure extricated himself from the dominance of nature and his instincts. His conscience knows of good and evil, and because of his self-awareness he has the freedom to decide. Yet that is only one side of him, for his life, his actions and ideas are moulded by archetypes, and the impulse to conquer unconsciousness is ingrained in the pre-existent self.

Man fulfils himself as its exponent, and fulfils himself equally as an autonomous ego-personality that creates meaning and self-awareness. Or to put it in other words: the self condemns him to bondage and destines him for freedom.[47]

Paul Tillich is alluding to this situation when he speaks of the "inescapability of freedom".[48] Every moment, whether we act or do not act, we are compelled to decide, at loggerheads with our own nature. Consequently there is a demand for freedom which causes the "profoundest unrest in our being . . . our whole being is threatened by it",[49] for it is not a matter of indifference how we decide. The necessity of decision hangs like a threat over our existence, nothing offers any certainty, not even—now—orthodoxy, piety or religious truth. In this radical exposure, with no safeguards, to the borderline situation of "inescapable freedom" Tillich sees the authentic hallmark of the Protestant.

Man is also "condemned to freedom" in the existentialist world of Sartre. Freedom hangs over him like doom. He is his own master, condemned to create himself. "I am condemned to have no other law but my own" (*The Flies*).[50] For existentialism, there is no agent outside the world of consciousness, no God for man to submit to, no self to destine him for freedom. In the end he is thrown back on himself, on his ego: as an ego he creates himself. In his insecurity and condemnation to utter freedom he finds his vocation. According to Tillich, the courage for this freedom is a "courage of despair", in which he nevertheless glimpses the possibility of finally conquering the fear of life.

From the psychological point of view all this leaves out of account the complementary fact that man as an ego-personality originated from the transcendental self, that all the time he is living by virtue of his ego's connection with its numinous origin whether he knows it or not.[51] Jung's words "It is not I

who create myself, rather I happen to myself"[52] posit the self
as an *a priori* existent. Whether known or unknown, it is the
hidden operator behind our lives. In the religious language of
the ancients: *Vocatus atque non vocatus Deus aderit*.[53] Called or
uncalled, affirmed or denied, the god will be present. Man
cannot escape being destined by the self even in his freedom,
but the possibility of an experience of meaning lies in recognising its imprint. Then his life becomes transpicuous to the
hidden imprinter.

Freedom and bondage accompany and condition the evolutionary
history of man. His consciousness has considerably increased in
scope since its first awakening and has acquired a strong sense
of freedom. Because of his rational enlightenment, his technology and scientific knowledge, civilised man is very much freer
than the so-called primitive, who is held captive, but also safe-
guarded, by nature and unconsciousness. Consciousness, expanding in the course of millennia, is the supreme prize of
evolution, not least because of the sense of freedom it conveys.
Yet the price paid was not small, for with his increasing self-
awareness and sense of freedom the original security and the
reliability of instinct got lost. Man became alienated from
nature, his consciousness forgot its origin in the unconscious,
and this one-sidedness became a source of violations of instinct
that lead to aberration, suffering, and once again to bondage —
quite apart from the fact that his original dependence on the
untamed forces of nature was replaced by an ever-growing
dependence on politics, industry and technology, with the
result that modern man, for all his freedom, is incapable of
resisting the suggestive influence of mass movements and all too
easily succumbs to them.

One-sided overvaluation of rational consciousness and of an
ego-dominated world, as well as vitiation of instinct, lie at the

root of many neuroses and psychic illnesses in modern man. Regard for and experience of the psychic background are thus an imperative necessity. It is one of the tasks of individuation for modern man to recognise that his autonomous consciousness, which fancies itself so superior and yet is so suggestible, is dependent on external social conditions as well as being determined by inner psychic factors and, in spite of this insight, to retain his sense of responsibility and freedom. The conscious personality, obeying its individual destiny, is the only bulwark against the mass movements of modern society. Herein lies the 'social meaning of individuation.

# 7

## GOOD AND EVIL

### *The Human Conflict*

The interweaving of freedom and bondage affects man most deeply in the conflict of good and evil. Am I free to choose good? Am I, without being responsible for it, condemned to do evil? Without the sense of inner freedom and without the autonomy of the ego there would be no individuation, neither would there be ethical action, nor meaning. For this reason, Jung attached crucial importance to conscience and responsibility. Confrontation with one's own darkness in analysis cannot take place without an alert conscience.

Jung's thoughts on the reality and effect of evil run like a red thread through his work. Though he studied evil as a psychic reality in the life of the individual and society, he was quite as much concerned with its numinous power and the part it plays in religion.[1] In the present context we must confine ourselves to those aspects which affect the question of meaning: Is meaning invalidated by evil? And is the meaning of individuation accomplished only if evil is condemned, if, in accordance with the Christian commandment, the goal is to eschew evil?

Jung answered no to both questions put in this absolute way; for the "powers of the left and right"[2] belong to wholeness, and the goal of individuation is not the perfect man but the complete man with his light and darkness. Evil as well as good is given to man along with the gift of life. It can never be completely conquered, yet man has a chance to hold it in check through self-awareness and struggle, and through confronting it

G

directly. The more conscious he is of his proclivities for evil, the more he is in a position to hold out against the destructive forces within him.

Individuation begins as a rule with becoming conscious of one's shadow, the unconscious darkness and evil that are yet an integral part of one's wholeness. In the shadow dwells everything that will not, or cannot, adapt itself to custom and convention as well as to religious and civil laws. It is the Mephistophelian negation, the counter-reality with its disobedience, recalcitrant will, and revolt against the cultural canon. A confrontation with the shadow is, none the less, rendered uncommonly difficult by the fact that it is not always and not unequivocally evil. The shadow is not destructive only, and conscience is not always on the side of the moral codex, for which we shall presently adduce two examples.

Because of this psychological complication a man's ethical attitude is an indispensable precondition of any confrontation with the shadow. But even for the ethical personality, or perhaps for it in particular, there are difficult or tragic situations in life when, against all reason and will, and in defiance of consciousness, conscience sides with the shadow, the inferior personality, and questions the value of conforming to the moral code. In situations like this the unity of the personality falls apart. Instead of a wholehearted affirmation of the generally accepted tradition, an individual conflict supervenes with all its suffering. We get, as Jung puts it, into a collision of duties. Obligation is pitted against obligation, will against will.

Jung found himself in just such a collision of duties when he left Freud, his teacher and fatherly friend. His decision to separate from Freud was preceded by long inner struggles. He took it out of obedience to the voice of conscience and to his destiny, but in disobedience to, or revolt against, the laws of filial duty, loyalty, respect and gratitude. His suffering and

disorientation in the years that followed the separation prove
how difficult this decision was. In any case it amounted to a
sacrifice.[3] It was only very much later that his life and work
demonstrated that it had not been made in vain.

Another example, taken from religious history and of far-
reaching significance, was the experience of Martin Luther who,
as an unknown young monk tormented by conscience, launched
forth into public criticism of the Catholic Church. The famous
words that are put into his mouth: "Here I stand, I can do no
other, so help me God, Amen," with which he ended his
defence at the Diet of Worms (1521), bear witness to the
agony of disobeying in order to obey.[4]

Collisions of duty are landmarks on the way of individuation,
for "nothing so promotes the growth of consciousness as this
inner confrontation of opposites".[5] They presuppose a responsible consciousness that is more differentiated than the obedient
observance of the law requires. A man's self-awareness and
ethics are tested not in the matter-of-fact fulfilment of secular
and spiritual precepts, but in the way he behaves and decides
when confronted with collisions of duty. Here he is challenged
as a whole man, standing alone. "In his case the court is transposed to the inner world where the verdict is pronounced behind
closed doors."[6]

It would be a disastrous mistake if we were to conclude from
the subtle interrogation of conscience demanded by Jung that
he is holding out a *carte blanche* to evil for subjective reasons.
"Even on the highest peak we shall never be 'beyond good and
evil' . . . for, as in the past, so in the future the wrong we have
done, thought or intended will wreak its vengeance on our
souls, no matter whether we turn the world upside down or
not."[7] The retroactive effect of evil makes itself felt in the
highest degree when it is not simply a matter of doing wrong
but of a genuine crime. As a psychiatrist, Jung found more

than once that, even if undiscovered and unatoned for, it can
have devastating effect on the soul and life of the doer.[8]

Yet something does change after all with the expansion of
consciousness: the naïve certainty in passing value judgments
gets lost. Outside the realm of self-evident moral demands,
"good" and "evil" lose their sharp contours: "In the last resort
there is no good that cannot produce evil and no evil that
cannot produce good."[9] Moreover, good and evil are not
absolutes but are man-made judgments, dependent on culture
and religion and on the feeling for values they impress upon us.
In consequence of this relativeness and uncertainty, the resolution of a moral conflict can no longer be decided by consciousness alone, nor by the traditional moral code; the inner voice
has also to be heard 'and the reaction of the unconscious taken
seriously. Individual responsibility is indeed owed to the world
without, but just as much to the world within and its highest
authority, the self.[10]

### Will and Counter-Will in the God-Image

Man's wholeness unfolds in the voluntary and conscious
endurance of the conflict, in its resolution by a decision to
act or refrain from acting. The cause of his being pulled in
two directions, torn between yes and no, will and counter-will,
good and evil, lies in the archetype of the transcendental self,
where the opposites are preformed in potentia. What constitutes
an invisible unity in the self appears in consciousness as a
dichotomy; split into two parts, it can be cognised. The ego
then experiences and suffers the antinomy of transconscious
wholeness in the form of complementary opposites.

The significance of the confrontation with moral opposites
can be fully gauged only when the religious aspect of wholeness,
its indistinguishability from the God-image in the psyche, is
taken into account alongside the psychological aspect. Though

this does not alter the facts, the way we express them alters, because we must now say that the yes and the no, the will and the counter-will, good and evil are contained in the God-image itself. In religious or metaphorical language, "our 'counter-will' is also an aspect of God's will".[11] Therefore God demands not only obedience of man, but also disobedience; it was God himself who gave man the "power to will otherwise".[12] This insight helps him to withstand a collision of duties or to solve a moral conflict.

In view of the moral conflict and the disconcerting, indeed stupefying, requirement that we disobey God, freedom and bondage are relativised in ethical action too. Here again the operative factor is the archetype of the self pushing into consciousness in order to bring its antinomian aspects into reality. They appear in religious imagery and doctrine as the moral ambivalence of the God-image, occasionally also as precepts regarding the attitude of the devout, who should have equal respect for both good and evil. Thus, in Rabbinic psychology, we meet with the doctrine of the two "inclinations" (*yeser*), and the injunction that man should love God with both of them. Zwi Werblowsky writes: " 'Two inclinations did the Holy One, blessed be He, create; the one is the good inclination, the other is the evil inclination' (B. Berakoth 61a). The inner man is nothing but the battleground of these two inclinations . . . The commandment: 'Thou shalt love the Lord thy God with all thine heart' is interpreted by the Misnah[13] as 'with both thine inclinations'."[14] Rabbinic psychology recognises that the Lord is the creator of the good and the evil inclinations, for it is said in Isaiah 45:7: "I form the light, and create darkness; I make peace, and create evil; I the Lord do all these things."

The conception of evil as a metaphysical reality in God was reformulated and developed further in the mysticism of the

Kabbala.[15] Good and evil are said to be lodged in God himself, severity shines forth side by side with his love. Or again, good and evil "interlock" in God, so that in evil, too, there is a spark of divine light shining. The root of all evil is said to lie in the very nature of Creation, so that everything hidden in God may be made fully manifest (Isaac Luria). The numerous attempts of Kabbalistic mysticism to explain the mystery of good and evil as a problem inherent in divinity itself can be traced back, according to Gershom Scholem, to "that prodigious turmoil which the Book of Job brought into the world, with its impassioned cross-examination of God".[16]

Today, nearly two and a half millennia later, that impassioned cross-examination of God has lost nothing of its urgency; as will be seen, it was the same "prodigious turmoil" that gripped Jung as he wrote his *Answer to Job*.

The moral ambivalence of a God who "makes peace and creates evil" also played a role in the history of Christianity, above all with Jakob Böhme (1575–1624). For him God's love and God's wrath, his glorious light and burning fire, belong inseparably together. Both are the "effluence of God's eternal word".[17] Böhme's prolific writings all bear the stamp of this revelation of God's incomprehensible polarity. "How is he a wrathful jealous God because he is himself immutable love? How can love and wrath be one thing?"[18] In Böhme's view good and evil are existential necessities. Life can only be when evil exists together with good, both in God and in man.[19]

The psychology of the unconscious expresses the same thought in another way: we experience the transconscious self through its good and evil effects. The evil effects manifest themselves as the shadow in our own psyche, but also as injustice and suffering in life and the world. Good and evil are aspects of the archetypal God-image and together make up the wholeness of man and of existence itself.

# 8

## ANSWER TO JOB

### Verbal Image and Object

Jung's demonstration of the moral antinomy of the self, especially when considered in its religious aspect as the moral antinomy of the God-image, outraged many of his readers and provoked violent resistance. The reactions might have been less violent had he based his proof simply on the manifestations of the unconscious in his patients or on works of profane literature. It would then have been less provocative. But he based it above all on an interpretation of the Book of Job and the Revelation of St John. This was misunderstood as an attack or a challenge. Since, from the psychological standpoint, Biblical writings must be taken as *documents humains*, as psychic testimonies of man, and since religious experience is a central reality of the psyche, Jung's statements remained within a psychological frame of reference; they did not, with their specific aims of research, encroach upon the realm of theology, nor did they touch upon the religious attitude of faith, which rests upon quite other foundations.

Jung read the Biblical text as a layman, without taking into account the findings of modern theological interpretations of the Bible. He took up this point in a letter (April 1960) to Dr Josef Rudin, S.J.: ". . . One more question! Is it in a tone of mild reproach that you say I take no account of 'Bible theology'? Had I done so I would have written from the theological standpoint, and you would have every right to accuse me of blasphemy. A similar accusation has been made from the Protestant side, that I disregard the higher textual criticism. But why haven't these gentlemen edited Job in such a way that it reads as it should, according to their view? I am a layman, and I have before me only the Job that has been served up to the lay public *cum consensu autoritatis*. It is about this Job that the layman thinks and not about the speculations of textual criticism, which he never gets a sight of anyway and which contribute nothing relevant to the spirit of this book . . ."[1]

For the lay reader the God described in the Book of Job has a dark and terrifying side. He doubts his pious servant Job and takes on a bet with Satan to put him to the test. He afflicts him with all manner of sufferings and tribulations and annihilates his household. "Riding along on the tempest of his almightiness he thunders reproaches at the half-crushed human worm."[2] The God of the Book of Job is unjust and cruel. He is a *tremendum*. The Christ of the Apocalypse is also a *tremendum*, meting out devastating punishment to mankind on the Day of Judgment. He too has a "terrible double aspect".[3]

In so far as the Book of Job deals with the image of a personal God, Jung speaks anthropomorphically of his "amoral side". Those are harsh words. Yet the charge of blasphemy levelled against him and his book misses both its content and its intention. Jung was not speaking of God himself, nor could he possibly speak of him. God himself—Tillich's "God beyond God"—is far removed from human depiction and far beyond man's grasp. He remains a *mysterium*. Jung's book is concerned with the specific *God-image* that emerges from the Book of Job, and the specific *Christ-image* that emerges from the Apocalypse. Yet the extraordinary numinosity of these and other religious images "is such that they not only give one the feeling of pointing to the *Ens realissimum*, but make one convinced that they actually express it and establish it as a fact".[4] Subjectively, the experience of the archetypal God-image is an experience of God. Hence the difficulty of intellectual discrimination and psychologically based scientific reflection.

If Jung nevertheless uses the word "God" or "divinity", it is only a verbal image, a concept or symbol,[5] regardless of whether he is taking over the common usage or the actual wording of the text he is interpreting, or has in mind the autonomy and numinosity of the archetype of the self. "When I say 'God' I mean an anthropomorphic (archetypal) God-image and do not imagine I have said anything about God," he wrote in a letter (April 1952). It must be admitted that this *sous-entendu* in the use of the word does not assist understanding and has led to all sorts of misconceptions. From the epistemological standpoint —which Jung is referring to here—the same *sous-entendu* exists for everyone who utters the word "God". We are incapable of expressing God himself, because as soon as we speak we use the traditional images of our language. Consequently, all talk about God is symbolic or mythological. Regardless of certain formulations to which we have already referred, the basis of all Jung's statements about religion is that God himself cannot be captured by any human words and descriptions or by any categories of value. "Good and evil are feeling-values of human provenance, and we cannot extend them beyond the human realm. What happens beyond this is beyond our judgment: God is not to be caught with human attributes."[6] Human attributes and moral categories of value apply only to the God-image.

For Jung, abolition of the identity of verbal image and object, appearance and reality, is necessary for the advance of human consciousness. This advance has already been made by science, as we have seen.[7] But Jung required it also of religious and theological thinking. "I have this advance of human con- sciousness particularly at heart", he wrote to a Protestant theologian (June 1955). "It is a difficult task to which I have devoted all my life's work." As we have seen, the differentiation of archetypal images in consciousness from the trans-conscious archetype *per se*, of the phenomenon from the noumenon, the imprint from the imprinter, lies at the root of his psychology of the unconscious.

### The Antinomy of the Holy (Paul Tillich)

In comparison with the paradox of the *numinosum*, what is commonly called "divine", namely goodness and grace, is something very one-sided. Tillich also puts forward this view in his philosophy of religion: "In its original sense the Holy denotes equally the divine and the daemonic. But as soon as the dichotomy of religious consciousness characterises the daemonic as daemonic, the idea of the Holy is equated with the divine. The Holy immediately becomes what is right, what is demanded."[8]

Tillich declares the antinomy of the divine the necessary precondition of its reality. "Self-affirmation of being without non-being would not even be self-affirmation but a fixed and immoveable self-identity. Nothing would be manifest, nothing expressed, nothing revealed ... Without the negative God has to overcome in himself and in his creatures, his positive self-affirmation would be a dead letter. There would be no revelation of the ground of being, there would be no life ... It is a symbolic language we are using here. But its symbolic character does not diminish its truth; on the contrary, it is a condition of its truth. To speak in non-symbolic language about being-itself would be untrue."[9]

The Book of Job uses symbolic language—in Tillich's sense as in Jung's—when it speaks of Job's hope of finding in God a helper and an "advocate" against God.[10] It is in symbolic language that Jung describes the "will to do otherwise" as

God's will, and the God of Job as good and evil. But when he points out the "ambivalence of the God-image", he is using scientific, non-symbolic language. Psychologically speaking, only an ambivalent God-image is genuinely monotheistic as in it "morally contradictory opposites exist side by side";[11] whereas identification of the divine with the good disregards one side of the numinous reality—evil, Tillich's the "dae-monic". This side created its own symbolic exponent in the figure of Satan, or the devil.[12]

These considerations led Jung to reject the Catholic doctrine of God as the *Summum Bonum* and he never withdrew his criticism. Here again he took the doctrine, and the definition of evil as a *privatio boni* (diminution of good) which was derived from it, literally and as a layman, just as he did the Book of Job, interpreting it psychologically on this basis. Modern theological exegesis of scholastic doctrines interested him just as little as theological excursions into "scientific" textual criticism of the Bible. The essential point for him was always the mythological and archetypal content of religious assertions. What interested him was the aboriginal elements underlying popular belief, and their psychological background. Thus there could be no compromise with Catholic theology in regard to the doctrine of the *privatio boni*.[13]

### Jung's Subjective Testament

The commonest reproach that *Answer to Job* is sarcastic in tone and emotional in language cannot be rebutted. There are long passages that are charged with emotion, ironic and aggressive. Jung was aware of this himself. At the outset he explains his style as a "purely subjective reaction" giving expression to the "shattering emotion which the unvarnished spectacle of divine savagery and ruthlessness produces in us", and for which the Book of Job "serves as a paradigm".[14]

The personal roots of Jung's subjective reaction go back to his childhood when, as a twelve-year-old boy, he experienced the evil and daemonic as an overwhelming reality. For many days and nights he wrestled with the darkness that welled up in himself until he overcame his fear. His courage in finding out the truth about the *tremendum* led unexpectedly to an experience of grace.[15] In addition, he had to look on helplessly while his father, a clergyman, went to pieces because of unresolved problems of faith. From then on the Christian conception of a kind and loving God could no longer be reconciled with Jung's religious feelings and his own psychic reality. The fact that, besides his father, eight of his uncles were parsons undoubtedly tipped the scales towards the compensatory dark side with such a reflective and introverted boy.

However, *Answer to Job* has to be understood as more than just a subjective reaction. All Jung's work is to a certain extent autobiographical. "My life is what I have done, my scientific work; the one is inseparable from the other. The work is the expression of my inner development; for the commitment to the contents of the unconscious forms the man and produces his transformations. My works can be regarded as stations along my life's way."[16] As an expression of inner development, as a station of the individuation process, *Answer to Job* is a confrontation between ego and self carried to the limits of the endurable; or to put it another way: what mattered most to Jung was his encounter with the Judaeo-Christian God-image. "God is always specific and always locally valid, otherwise he would be ineffectual. The Western God-image is the valid one for me, whether I assent to it intellectually or not. I do not go in for religious philosophy, but am held in thrall, almost crushed, and defend myself as best I can," Jung wrote to Erich Neumann in a letter (January 1952) about *Answer to Job*. He wrestled with the immediacy of religious experience. His emotional thraldom—in the same letter he calls it "barbaric, infantile and abysmally unscientific"—is an expression of the subjugation of the ego under the overwhelming might of the self, concretised in the God-image.

Jung's sarcasm, for which he has been widely censured, has to be understood in the light of this psychic situation: it was a defence mechanism against the assault of the archetype, against the "God" who held him in thrall. As he wrote to a theologian (November 1951): "Sarcasm is certainly not a pretty quality, but I am forced to use even means I find reprehensible in order to deliver myself from the Father . . . Sarcasm is the means with which we hide our hurt feelings from ourselves, and from this you can see how very much the knowledge of God has wounded me, and how very much I would have preferred to remain a child in the Father's protection . . ."

The common estimate of *Answer to Job* is that it is an impassioned and ruthless attack on the God of the Old Testament, but psychologically considered it is an attempt to come to terms with the numinous image of the self and its "shattering reality".[17] Subjective experience does not discriminate and is incapable of discrimination. What counts subjectively is the emotional thraldom, and not the differentiation and labelling of that which holds one in thrall. For Jung, of course, the "shattering reality" became an occasion for objective reflection as well as historical and psychological research. Emotion and scientific conscience held a precarious balance in this confrontation with the numinous contents of the deepest layers of the psyche.

Seesawing between feeling and thinking, religious passion and scientific objectivity, *Answer to Job* is the most dynamic of Jung's books. The human factor stands out most; the book is a religious and personal testament. Jung had avoided the confrontation for years. It has a long prehistory that can be traced back to his early writings. It needed, as he himself admitted, a severe illness to break down his resistance. During the illness there rose to the surface, now irresistible, the contents of the unconscious by which he was "impregnated". Scarcely recovered, he worked them over and wrote the book down at a single draft. "If there is anything like the spirit seizing one by the scruff of the neck, it was the way this book came into being," he says in a letter (July 1951).

### The World's Suffering

*Answer to Job* is, however, not sufficiently explained by taking it merely as a personal testament. For the self is not just an individual entity, it is a collectively valid archetype, and the same is true when it appears as a God-image. So, too, Jung's concern with it was not personal merely, nor even historical, but was directed as well to the spiritual situation of modern man. "We have experienced things so unheard of and so staggering that the question of whether such things are in any way reconcilable with the idea of a good God has become burningly topical. It is no longer a problem for experts in theological seminaries, but a universal religious nightmare, to the solution of which even a layman in theology like myself can, or perhaps must, make a contribution."[18] The autobiographical element recedes into the distance, and it is from this vantage point that *Answer to Job* has to be understood.

"How can God allow these things?" "Is there still a God?" Such are the despairing questions raised by the unspeakable suffering that has engulfed mankind. The silence of resignation, disgust with religion, political and philosophical nihilism, cynicism, indifference, spiritual emptiness are the typical reactions of suffering humanity. No one can blame them, though they do not give an answer to the primary questions. But in the psyche there lies an archetypal image of "shattering reality" that does contain the answer. It is the God-image with its "terrible double aspect". Faced with this image, including evil within itself as a *tremendum*, a new gospel holds good, which Jung calls the eternal as distinct from the temporal: "*one can love God but must fear him*".[19] When the Old Testament fear of God reappears side by side with the love promised in the New, we need no longer stand aghast before the atrocities which life and fate prepare for us now and in the future. The abysms and glories of life, of good and evil, are evidence of a transcendental reality beyond our grasp, though we experience its effects in their full intensity and have its image graven in the soul. Psychology speaks of it as the self, synonymous with divinity, which, refracted in the individual, constitutes the wholeness of our being and the wholeness of life, and "arranges" the mutually antagonistic experiences life throws in our path. They are actualisations of the self's paradoxical nature.

Yet even the "new gospel" and insight into the self will not eliminate the world's suffering, for evil is one of Creation's mysteries which will endure as long as life endures. There is no "banality of evil", as Hannah Arendt thinks; but at the nadir of torment, when life is darkened by suffering, horror and all wickedness, it still points to something beyond itself. Beyond consciousness, and at its very source, the God-image appears in its "terrible double aspect". The possibility of transcendence, of reuniting the darkness of life with its numinous origin, even at the price of being shattered by the *tremendum*, can be the beginning of inner liberation. Job found a meaning in the tragic ruin of his life, and with it peace and redemption, when God revealed himself in all his monstrous antinomy. Will Job ever cease to exist—the man tested by God, the victim of incomprehensible evil?

Jean Améry, a Jewish writer and member of the Belgian Resistance, who spent two years in concentration camps including Auschwitz, and was tortured, gives an account[20] of an experience he never expected to happen to him: in the border-line situations of extreme suffering, the spirit that had kept him alive, and that he counted on, turned into something totally unreal. It collapsed in the face of reality. For him and other intellectuals in the camps, the abomination of desolation knocked the bottom out of their "philosophical inventory", their aesthetic and artistic feelings dwindled to nothing, all spiritual interests gave way to complete indifference. What meaning could his favourite poems of Hölderlin have amid the fearful reality of Auschwitz? The spirit, the spirit of the philosopher and fine-drawn intellectual, suddenly lost its most fundamental quality, the power of transcendence.

But with faith it was different. When it was a genuine faith, it endured. Believers possessed something that carried them through every suffering, they were able to transcend themselves and reality, regardless of whether it was a religious or metaphysical belief or an immanent one, say in a political party. In Améry's experience a living faith was not destroyed even when suffering touched the depths. On the contrary, the believer "belongs to a spiritual continuum that is nowhere interrupted, not even in Auschwitz".[21]

We know today of other examples—the brave Protestant Dietrich Bonhoeffer, who was killed in a concentration camp, and of interned Catholics who celebrated Mass amid the unthinkable difficulties of camp life. Above all, we know of God-fearing Jews, too countless to number, who chanted the prayers in the camps and, tortured by raging hunger, yet kept the fast on the Day of Atonement, and went to their death in the gas chambers singing "Hear, O Israel".

Améry, a self-confessed intellectual and agnostic, even in his suffering could not bring himself to avow any faith although he had a convincing image of its indestructibility and durability before his eyes. The reason for his incapacity: "All talk of the inexhaustible goodness of God seemed to me a scandal."[22]

Jung did not write in the first place for believers, the "*beati possidentes*" as he called them, the happy possessers of an everlasting truth. He addressed himself to those who were unable to believe but wanted to *know*, even if knowledge, by its very nature, has to halt at a frontier. Because he acknowledged the splendour and darkness of the numinous, the inexhaustible goodness of God and the divine fire of destruction as antinomian aspects of a single whole, and had the courage to show up the paradoxicality of the self and of God-images, making us aware of the complementary existence of a dark chthonic spirit alongside the spirit of light, he drew heavy fire on himself from his critics. But he also got any number of grateful, affirmative reactions from people who felt liberated. Unlike the others, these reactions generally came from people who belonged to no creed because they could not believe or could do so no longer, from young people and "the man in the street". It was these that pleased Jung most.

In spite or perhaps because of the ambivalence of the God-image, Jung left the question of meaning or meaninglessness open. The intensity and unfathomability of evil, revealed in such unspeakable ways by man, prompted him, as we said at the beginning, to confess in old age: "I cherish the anxious hope that meaning will preponderate and win the battle."[23] Here the certainty of knowing had reached the point of no return.

H

# 9

## THE INDIVIDUATION OF MANKIND

### *The God-Image of the Holy Ghost*

The self, being individual and unique, is made manifest in the individuation process of the individual. But the self is also universal and eternal, and under this aspect it is made manifest in a process we can only call the individuation of mankind. It is a collective process that takes the form of a gradual extension and differentiation of consciousness over the millennia. The drama "began in the grey mists of antiquity and continues through the centuries into a remote future. This drama is an 'Aurora Consurgens'—the dawning of consciousness in mankind."[1] As far back as historical records go, it is accompanied by a continually changing conception of God or of the God-image: "The gods at first lived in superhuman power and beauty on the top of snow-clad mountains or in the darkness of caves, woods, and seas. Later on they drew together into one god, and then that god became man."[2] Jung studied the collective process more particularly in the phase of the transformation of the Jewish into the Christian God-image and the way this developed into the Trinity, for the "life-process within the Deity",[3] as depicted in the Bible and in dogma, is of supreme relevance to the psyche of modern man.[4]

Personal individuation is not separate from collective individuation, since the spirit of the age realises itself in the individual and the specific, time-bound God-image is constellated in his unconscious as an image of totality, the self.

This image in the psyche of the Old Testament Jew is different from that of the early Christian or the man of today.[5] To anticipate: Jung recognised that the self which is constellated and being brought into reality in the psyche of modern man corresponds to the God-image of the Holy Ghost, the final efflorescence of the Christian conception of God. He based this on his interpretation of Biblical writings and dogmas, which were for him "repositories of the secrets of the soul, and this matchless knowledge is set forth in grand symbolical images".[6]

Here again Jung was careful to distinguish between verbal image and object, this being his epistemological and philosophical premise. As we have seen, it led him to distinguish God himself (the unknowable object) from the knowable God-image[7] (the verbal image in Bible and dogma), just as, in psychology, he made the corresponding conceptual distinction between the irrepresentable archetype of the self and its concretisations in archetypal images. The unfathomability of God and the unfathomability of the self account for the synonymity, not identity, of the two concepts.

With these correlations in mind, the interaction of ego and self, which we discussed earlier—their autonomy and freedom on the one hand and their mutual dependence on the other—can also be formulated as the relation between man and God. It would then not be the case that the "ego arises out of the self" or the "self emerges into consciousness seeking actualisation", but we would have to say in religious language that "God creates man" or "God seeks man and actualises himself in encountering his creature". Likewise, it would not be true that the "self is created by the consciousness which discerns it and which is deepened by this discernment", but rather "God is revealed by man" or "man's consciousness is deepened by its encounter with God". Let it be emphasised once more that a psychological approach can never quite refrain from reverting to the original religious verbal images. The archetypal contents rising up from the unconscious have an emotional charge, a numinosity, that ought not to be lost but must constantly be called back into memory again. Then only does the reality of the psyche reveal its depth.

The reciprocal relation between man and God (psychologically, between ego-consciousness and self) is the focus of development of the Judaeo-Christian God-image over the centuries, which Jung dates from the Book of Job. Job became conscious of the "oppositeness" in God—in other words, the antinomy of the God-image—and this insight made him, a mere mortal, superior to the *tremendum*. This unprecedented transposition of values resulted in a transformation of the image under which the *numinosum* appeared: God himself became man. Or, as Jung puts it, God's incarnation is the answer to Job.[8]

Psychologically, "incarnation" is a symbol of becoming conscious; the self penetrates deeper into man's expanded consciousness, is actualised in new form, and a new aeon begins in history. "Yahweh's decision to become man is a symbol of the development that had to supervene when man becomes conscious of the sort of God-image he is confronted with."[9]

This transformation of the relation of man to God, or ego-consciousness to self, is psychologically based on the equilibrium of a continually changing potential between these two interacting entities. At one moment the self overpowers ego-consciousness and forcibly brings about its transformation and expansion; at another, ego-consciousness undergoes a mutation and penetrates deeper into the unconscious thanks to its powers of cognition. In both cases man is transformed and so is the God-image. Yet it can never be established with certainty which came first and what was the result. In Job's case the

THE INDIVIDUATION OF MANKIND    115

possibility cannot be excluded that the process was initiated
in the unconscious by the self, and that God, driven as it were
by a secret longing for more consciousness, sought that
encounter with the mortal man.

It is exceedingly difficult, if not impossible, for an orthodox
believer to rethink religious concepts that have been valid for
centuries (God, Christ, Holy Ghost, etc.) as verbal images
which, though pointing to their transcendental referent, should
not be confused with it; for faith and scientific psychology
approach their object in diametrically opposite ways. They
seem to meet only in the symbolic relation of Christ to self,
because since St Paul the conception of the "Christ within" has
found its place in Christian thinking, with the result that we
have become more conscious also of its psychological and archetypal aspect. What seems to be the strangest of all is the
psychological approach to the Holy Ghost, even when the
third Person of the Trinity is expressly understood not as a
metaphysical entity but as a verbal image. It is possible that
the feeling of strangeness stems not only from the discovery
of its archetypal background but from the difficulty in understanding its mystery, in addition to which the role the Holy
Ghost plays in Christian thinking is not nearly as great as that
of God the Father and God the Son.

Jung attached special importance to the symbolism of the
Holy Ghost, because he saw in it a starting-point for the
further development and reactivation of the Christian myth,[10]
which falls on increasingly deaf ears. "Christianity slumbers
and has neglected to develop its myth further in the course of
the centuries . . . Our myth has become mute, and gives no
answers."[11] This protest of Jung's is scattered throughout his
works, since he had found as a doctor how gravely the loss
of the myth affects the psyche.

The symbolism of the Holy Ghost is important for the future development of Christianity, and also from the psychological point of view, because it draws man into the "life-process within the Deity". Christ promised to send the Holy Ghost to his disciples as the Paraclete ("Counsellor") after his death—and not only to them but to mankind also, to "procreate in man and bring forth works of divine parentage".[12] Jung saw it as a symbolic event of the utmost importance that the apostles, who were mortal men, and after them the creaturely and guilt-laden human race too should become vessels of the Holy Ghost, who by definition is a spirit consubstantial with God. Christ was the first man in whom God incarnated, but Christ was more divine than human, he was begotten by the Holy Ghost, born of a mother immaculately conceived, was consubstantial with the Father and remained without sin. The indwelling of the Holy Ghost in the ordinary man creates a new and closer relationship between God and his creature. Jung speaks of a "continuing incarnation"[13] and draws the conclusion: God wanted and wants to become man, then, now, and in the future.

In the archetypal image of "God in man" the symbolism of the self and the symbolism of the Holy Ghost join hands; for the continuing incarnation of God and the indwelling of the Holy Ghost in mortal man correspond, God and self being synonymous, to the indwelling of the self and its realisation in the individual. The dawning of consciousness in man is, metaphysically speaking, a "part of the divine life-process",[14] and the Holy Ghost must be understood as "the self's actualisation in man".[15]

In Christ, God incarnated his good side. Hence, in the Christian myth, the primary opposites, good and evil, remain irreconcilable: the non-incarnated evil confronts Christ in the figure of Satan, the eternal adversary.[16] The reason for this partial incarnation lies in the boundlessness of the self, which can be assimilated into consciousness only gradually and never in its entirety. In addition, the boundless force of inertia opposes the desire for transformation and greater consciousness. It is the same in individual life: everyone who struggles to individuate and become more conscious is thwarted by this inhibiting and decelerating tendency in the unconscious. "The unconscious wants to flow into consciousness in order to reach the light, but at the same time it continually thwarts itself, because it would rather remain unconscious. That is to say, God wants to become man, but not quite."[17] Or: God seeks man and withdraws from him.

In the course of individuation good and evil, light and shadow, are recognised as aspects of the transcendental self. It is therefore a precondition of individuation that life should be lived to the full, and that man should become conscious of his guilt and his shadow. "The guilty man is eminently suited and is therefore chosen to become the vessel for the continuing incarnation, not the guiltless one who holds aloof from the world and refuses to pay his tribute to life, for in him the dark God would find no room."[18] The darkness of the shadow can be integrated without ill effects only if we have become sufficiently conscious of the light: the sense of one's own value should not get lost, darkness should not gain the upper hand. The incarnation of good is a necessary prelude if we are to hold out against evil. "We therefore need more light, more goodness and moral strength, and must wash off as much of the obnoxious blackness as possible, otherwise we shall not be able to assimilate the dark God who also wants to become man, and at the same time endure him without perishing. For this all the Christian virtues are needed and something else besides, for the problem is not only moral: we also need the Wisdom that Job was seeking."[19]

We have already discussed the collisions of duty in which life or the opposites in the self can embroil us. If the opus is successful, the realisation of opposites and the confrontation with them is followed by their reconciliation through experience of the self, a process that is constantly repeated in individuation and each time demands a renewed effort. The painful collisions of duty and the tensions between obedience and disobedience, freedom and bondage, conscious and unconscious can be resolved in the antinomy of the supraordinate self; it embraces the divine and the daemonic, creation and destruction, spirit and instinct, world and matter; it is "eternal and unitemporal", creator and created, origin and end. Every overcoming of opposites, every actualisation of the self, corresponds to a religious experience of the Holy Ghost and its realisation in man. For the God-image of the Holy Ghost, said on the highest authority to have been left behind for mortal man, likewise has a nature that unites the opposites. It is a "mute, eternal, unfathomable One in whom God's love and God's terribleness come together in wordless union."[20]

T. S. Eliot turned the paradoxical experience of "God's love and God's terribleness" into one of his most important poems. And since a work of art can also be understood as a statement about the events that set their stamp on the age, the dumbfounding image in the last of his *Four Quartets* can be considered a confirmation of their psychological counterpart: the *Luftwaffe*'s attack on London and the consequent conflagration are transmuted into the mystery of divine fire, blending the utmost torment with everlasting love. From the holocaust there rises up a vision of the dove of the Holy Ghost, flying down to earth with "flame of incandescent terror" to kindle the Pentecostal fire. "Who then devised the torment?" "Love". God's love weaves the flaming Nessus shirt of history, agonising yet not to be thrown off. But man is free to choose the flame either for damnation or purification:

> The only hope or else despair
> Lies in the choice of pyre and pyre—
> To be redeemed from fire by fire.

Hans Holthusen calls Eliot's verses a "shattering, dizzying paradox sprung from the depths of Christian wisdom".[21]

### Reconciling the Opposites in the God-Image

The goal of individuation is the synthesis of opposites, once they have become conscious, in the self. More accurately, it is the goal of individuation for modern man. For "in the experience of the self it is no longer the opposites 'God' and 'man' that are reconciled, as it was before, but rather the opposites within the God-image itself."[22] This reconciling process cannot take place without the co-operation of consciousness. Man is challenged to a task that transcends him and yet is his destiny. "The *mysterium coniunctionis* is the concern of man" (Letter, January 1952).

From the psychological standpoint, the reconciliation of opposites in the God-image would, for the first time, make a reality of Christian monotheism. Satan, the adversary, would no longer be, figuratively speaking, outside the Trinity, but would come together with it in "wordless union" to form a quaternity. Monotheistic God-images in this sense, which unite good and evil, are also known in the Judaeo-Christian sphere of religion. We have already mentioned the God-image of Jakob Böhme. Jung appealed chiefly to the Book of Job and, within Christianity proper, besides Böhme and Nicholas of Cusa (1401–64),[23] to the Church Father, Clement of Rome,[24] who "taught that God rules the world with a right and a left hand, the right being Christ, the left Satan. Clement's view is clearly *monotheistic* as it unites the opposites in one God."[25]

Whether it was a deepened consciousness that provided the impetus for a new transformation of the God-image in which the opposites were united, or whether the impulse came from the archetype of the self, it is impossible to determine. As with every transformation, conscious and unconscious participate in equal measure; it is a co-operation of self and man or, metaphorically speaking, God and man. Through their interaction the religious myth appears as the "revelation of a divine life in man",[26] and "man's achievement of consciousness as a part of the divine life-process".[27] The dynamism with which the archetype of the self forces its way into consciousness and the resultant response—the realisation of wholeness—reflect the image of a God who seeks man in order to become conscious of himself in him, and of his Creation in his creature. That God needs man, that he still seeks him in the torment of fire to which he condemns him, is an idea we find in the Old Testament. Isaiah 48:10–11: "Behold, I have refined thee, but not [as] silver; I have [tested] thee in the furnace of affliction. For mine own sake, even for mine own sake, will I do it." Jung quoted this passage in a letter (March 1955). But he set a limit to man's answer to the demand of the Almighty, for he continued: "Human understanding and will are challenged and can help, but they can never pretend to have plumbed the depths of the spirit and to have quenched the fire raging within it. We can only hope that God, in his grace, will not compel us to go deeper and let ourselves be consumed in his fire." In other words, the experience of God and the self is, as he wrote in another letter (June 1955), an "endless approximation". The goal remains hidden and unattainable.

The conscious realisation of the self as a paradoxical human whole and a paradoxical God-image was, for Jung, the cultural and religious task of modern man, constellated by the spirit of the age. With this we seem to have come full circle. The line of development returns to the initial state, when Job was confronted with the good and evil God-image. Yet a fundamental transformation of experience has taken place: Job projected its double aspect into a divine power outside man, whereas we recognise it as the paradoxical background of our own being and our fate. The morally ambivalent God-figure reveals itself as an image of the "God within", the self. Though God appears self-evident, he remains ungraspable and hidden, a mystery beyond all images and all attempts to describe him.

# 10

## MAN IN THE WORK
## OF REDEMPTION

Thanks to the dynamism of the archetype, the Old Testament God-image underwent a special development in later Judaism.[1] Ever since Job, Judaism had been faced with the question of good and evil, and of their meaning in relation to the God-image. But evil was never split off from it as it was in Christianity. Its antinomy persisted, and emerged even more plainly when it underwent further development and differentiation in the mysticism of the Kabbala. Jung conjectures that the Christian answer to this question, the unequivocal decision in favour of God's goodness, did not satisfy the conservative Jews in early Christian times and that they rejected the gospel for that reason.[2]

The role of man in the myth of the divine drama—the pivot for any psychological approach to religious statements—comes out most clearly in the Kabbala of Isaac Luria (1534–72). He describes in highly original, mystical images the divine life-process which man had to assist with all his powers.[3] Man is indispensable in the work of world redemption. According to Scholem's account the dramatic course of events was, briefly, as follows:

As the divine light poured into the mystical primordial space God had created or left free, vessels were made for the purpose of catching and conserving the individual rays of light, but proved too weak to hold them. The vessels burst asunder and the "fiendish nether worlds emerged from the fragments".[4] Since then everything that exists is inwardly fractured and carries within itself this flaw. Redemption, the secret goal of all development, consists in the restoration of the original harmony which was disturbed by the breaking of the vessels, a process that can also be conceived as the perfecting of God. The restitution of all things to their true status requires "not only an impulse from God but also one that comes from His creatures".[5] Man plays his part in the divine cosmic course of events when the inner purpose of all his actions is to restore the original unity; even his mystic meditation in prayer — a "descent to the deepest recesses of the soul"[6] — helps to "unify the name of God"[7] and to add "the final touch to the divine countenance".[8]

The co-operation of man in transforming and unifying God and in perfecting Creation corresponds in the psychological realm to the role of consciousness in developing the Judaeo-Christian God-image over the centuries. Here also the end or goal is the healing of the breach, the reconciliation or union of opposites in the God-image. Originally the opposites had a unity, even though this was unconscious. But with the growing differentiation of consciousness under Christianity they split apart as the light and dark sides of God — Christ and Satan — until, at the present point of the process, on a new level of development, they coalesce in the symbol of the Holy Ghost or of a quaternary God-image or, psychologically, in the self. This cannot be done without the help of man. "God is a contradiction in terms, therefore he needs man in order to be made one. God is an ailment man has to cure" (Letter, January 1952).

Isaac Luria's account of man's participation in the work of redemption was of the utmost significance for Jung. Indeed, he took it as evidence of the superiority of Kabbalistic thinking over the Christian view of the world. In answer to the question as to what the attitude of a Jew should be to Christ, he wrote to James Kirsch (February 1954):

"I scarcely think that the Jews have to accept the Christ symbol. They must only understand its meaning. Christ wanted to change Jahwe into a moral God of goodness, but in so doing he tore apart the opposites that were united in him though in an inharmonious and unconscious way (Satan falling from heaven, Luke 10:18), hence the suspension between opposites at the crucifixion. The purpose of the Christian reformation through Jesus was to eliminate the evil moral consequences that were caused by the amoral divine prototype. One cannot 'strain at a gnat and swallow a camel' (Matth. 23:24) or 'serve two masters' (Matth. 6:24) at the same time.

"This moral differentiation is a necessary step on the way of individuation. Without thorough knowledge of good and evil, ego and shadow, there is no recognition of the self, but at most an involuntary and therefore dangerous identification with it.

"The Jew has roughly the same moral development behind him as the Christian European, consequently he has the same problem. A Jew can recognise the *self* in that hostile pair of brothers, Christ and Satan, as well as I can or perhaps even better, and hence the incarnation or assimilation of Jahwe in man. Naturally the status of man is profoundly altered because of this.

"The Jew has the advantage of having long since anticipated the development of consciousness in his own mental history. By this I mean the Lurian stage of the Kabbala, the breaking of the vessels and man's help in restoring them. Here the thought emerges for the first time that man must help God to make good the mischief wrought by creation. For the first time the cosmic responsibility of man is acknowledged. Naturally it is a question here of the self and not the ego, although the latter is deeply affected.

"That is the answer I would give a Jew . . ."

The psychological involvement of man in the reality of religious statements and experiences reflects an epistemological view that is current in all sciences today. We know that man, through his psyche, influences the observation of the object; he is a co-determining factor of the phenomenal world. In everything he observes and in everything he investigates he meets himself (Heisenberg); even the physicist's theories and insights are organised by archetypal images in the unconscious, which Pauli calls "operators". Jung applied the relations he had investigated between subject and object, conscious and unconscious, ego and self to religious statements: under every revelation there lie autonomous archetypes as operators or ordering factors. Thus man encounters himself in the numinous transformations of the God-image too. But he encounters himself as the self, not as an ego. Religious myth is the "revelation of a divine life in man. It is not we who invent it, rather it speaks to us as a Word of God."[9] It should not be forgotten, however, that man also encounters himself in psychology, in its laws and images. Jung attached great importance to the consequences of this limitation. "The physicist's models ultimately rest on the same archetypal foundations that also underlie the speculations of the theologian. Both are psychology, and it too has no other foundation."[10] The archetypal foundation is the foundation of all cognition. It is the precondition of a unitary view of the world, in which the irreconcilability of the natural and social sciences, as well as of psychology and theology, is overcome. "There is only *one* reality" ran like a refrain through conversations with Jung and with Pauli.

Becoming conscious of the psychic background does not, as we have already said, mean any diminution of religious experience. On the contrary, man plunges into the midst of religious revelation. His experience then rests not on faith alone; he feels the reality of the God-image in its "compelling numinosity".[11] This experience underlies a letter Jung wrote to a Catholic theologian in January 1948: "I thank God every day that I have been permitted to experience the reality of the *imago Dei* in me. Had that not been so, I would be a bitter enemy of Christianity and of the Church in particular. Thanks to this *actus gratiae* my life has meaning, and my inner eye was opened to the beauty and grandeur of dogma."[12]

In immediate experience of the *numinosum*, and in deepening this experience through knowledge and understanding, Jung saw the possibility of renewing the Christian message and giving the dogma of the Trinity a wholly new topicality. In the history of religion his psychological approach to the dogma is a *novum*, and this is especially true of its corollary—the inclusion of man in the revelatory process. Jung seldom expressed an opinion on the importance of his discoveries. But his judgment stands out clearly in a letter to a young theologian (August 1953): "Just as Origen understood the Holy Scriptures as the body of the Logos, so we must also interpret the psychology of the unconscious as a phenomenon of assimilation. The Christ-image as we know it certainly did not appear as the result of human intervention, it was the transcendental ('total') Christ who created for himself a new and more specific body . . ." There is no need to point out that these words are not psychologism but refer to the changing modes of apprehending the indescribable. The impetus to create the "more specific" body is not given by man but comes from the transcendental Christ—in psychological terms, from the archetype in its "eternal presence".[13] Man, it must be added, experiences it and assimilates this experience by ceaselessly striving to penetrate the unfathomable and by his dialogue with the numinous contents of the unconscious.

# II

## THE ONE REALITY

Jung realised—and it was a rueful realisation—that his thoughts about a renewal of the Christian myth "lay a very heavy burden on the theological conscience",[1] and that they are only just beginning to gain a small measure of currency. In this connection he spoke, like Joachim of Flora (1135–1202), of an age of the Holy Spirit[2] which would succeed the stage of the Father in Judaism and of the Son in Christianity.[3] But whereas Joachim was a mystic for whom the Holy Spirit was a metaphysical reality, a divine creative force, Jung used the term as a symbol that at most gives a hint of its mystery, or as a verbal image that is accessible to scientific thought. The advance to this third stage he saw more particularly in an antinomian or paradoxical view of physical and psychic realities. He interpreted the all but incomprehensible sin against the Holy Ghost as man's one-sidedness against his better judgment.[4]

Pauli too considered that the "goal of overcoming the opposites in a synthesis embracing rational understanding as well as the mystic experience of oneness is the explicit or tacit myth of our time".[5] And the poet Gottfried Benn (1886–1956) declared, in surprisingly similar terms, that the "integration of ambivalence", by which he meant the "fusion of each and every concept with its counter-concept", was "the spiritual hallmark of our epoch".[6] One climax of the fusion of concept and counter-concept might be seen in the reconciliation of opposites in the God-image, which we have dealt with in the foregoing chapters.

This third stage has scarcely begun. It "points beyond the 'Son' into the future, to a continuing realisation of the 'spirit',"[7] or "a continuing operation of the Holy Ghost",[8] which at the same time preserves the vitality of the Christian tradition. Jung regarded the promulgation of the dogma of the Assumption of the Virgin in 1950 as just such a realisation of the spirit, as the recognition of a popular movement that had its counterpart in the unconscious and had long announced itself in dreams and visions.[9] He regarded the declaration of this dogma as "the most important religious event since the Reformation",[10] chiefly because it exalted the feminine and bodily principles[11] which were both excluded from the masculine and spiritual God-image of the Trinity. Thus the dogma of the Assumption may be seen, from the psychological standpoint, as a symbolic approximation of opposites: the masculine and the feminine, body and spirit. But for all his estimation of the dogma Jung nevertheless insisted on the right of constructive criticism, and this was in keeping with his Protestant turn of mind.

The necessity of reconciling religion and Eros, widely recognised today, has to be reviewed in this context. That the question is discussed at all is something of a turning-point. For centuries Christianity fought against the power of Eros and condemned it as sinful; whereupon, with increasing emancipation from the Church, a counter-movement set in, which in turn has led to an excessive sexualisation of life.[12] Neither then nor now was any contribution made to a realisation of the self, for this embraces both sides: spirit and body, Logos and Eros. Only when the alienation of Eros from the sacral realm has been halted can the wholeness and unity of man come to fruition.

The oecumenical movement too, in its attempt to bring together the various Christian denominations in a totality superior to them all, may be taken as a sign of a constellated trend towards unity. Though he took no active part, Jung sympathised with these endeavours, since he felt he owed allegiance to the Protestant and Catholic viewpoints equally. He felt himself first and foremost a Christian. In September 1944 he wrote to a Catholic critic: "I know little of Church doctrine, but this little is sufficient to make it something I can never lose, and I know so much of Protestantism that I could never give it up. This regrettable indecision is what you, with so much psychological acuity, censure as a 'complex'. Now as regards this indecision I must tell you that it is something I have consciously and deliberately decided upon. Since no man can serve two masters, I can submit neither to one creed nor the other, but only to the *one* that stands above the conflict. As Christ is eternally being sacrificed he hangs eternally between the two thieves. There are good Catholic and good Protestant Christians. The Church having suffered a schism, I must be satisfied with being a Christian who is in the same conflict Christianity is in. I cannot disavow my brother who, in good faith and for reasons I cannot invalidate with a good conscience, is of a different opinion . . ."[13]

A reconciliation of opposites is also making headway in science. Facts that before seemed incompatible are proving to be complementary aspects of the same totality. *"Contraria non contradictoria sed complementa sunt"*[14] is a saying Niels Bohr was fond of quoting. Pauli pointed out that to us "the only acceptable point of view appears to be one that recognises *both* sides of reality—the quantitative and the qualitative, the physical and the psychical—as compatible with each other, and can embrace them simultaneously".[15] For this reason he laid it down that besides "adjusting our knowledge to external objects (we should also) bring to light the archetypal images used in the creation of our scientific concepts"[16] He himself used Kepler as an example of the way the formation of scientific theories, particularly in physics, is influenced by archetypal forms and structures. Similarly, the social sciences now recognise the formative influence of unconscious images or "metaphysical factors" in history, politics, economics, state-craft, etc., while biology takes note of creative factors resembling archetypes in its study of living organisms. The fact that we can deduce the influence of unconscious archetypes on the processes of artistic creation and that archetypal dreams form a contrapuntal accompaniment to life has long been known. The growing regard for these unconscious, operative factors in all departments of life is bringing to light a pro-gressive approximation of those primal opposites, the inner and outer worlds.

Pauli espouses a standpoint that recognises the compatibility of physics and psychology in particular and seeks to unify them. It is also that of Jungian psychology. In 1935 C. A. Meier established that between modern physics and the psy-chology of the unconscious there is a "genuine and authentic relationship of complementarity".[17] For his part, Jung spoke of a "unity of their subject-matters". "Microphysics is feeling its way into the unknown side of matter, just as complex psychology is pushing forward into the unknown side of the psyche",[18] and he suggests that there is some probability that these two unknowns stand for the same transcendental reality. This is a theme on which much research is being done to-day.[19]

In medicine this unifying tendency shows itself especially in psychosomatics, for which the traditional opposites "body and mind" are complementary aspects of a single whole. This whole too is transcendental and therefore indescribable. In

1926 Jung, recognising the possibility of a body-mind unity, spoke of an "unknowable living being, concerning the ultimate nature of which nothing can be said except that it vaguely expresses the quintessence of life".[20]

With regard to the human condition today, the reconciliation of opposites is a goal that still lies in the distant future. In spite of all our knowledge and all our striving for unity, the world is split apart in ideological dichotomy, science is fragmented, and man suffers from psychic dissociation. This is the suffering that Jungian psychology, in its practical work, seeks to heal or at least to palliate. It encourages man to make himself conscious of the opposites within him, and to surmount and unite them in a synthesis; in the individuation process it fosters the development of an inner unity corresponding to an antinomian or paradoxical God-image.

Jung added a new dimension to the unitary view of the world that is being sought of necessity today. He took a step beyond modern research; for though this recognises body and mind or matter and spirit as aspects of the same reality, he held that the religious element was an indispensable element in the total picture. The natural and social sciences were confronted with the reality of an irrepresentable background, an abyss of mystery, which exerts a formative influence on world events and organic life-processes as well as on the creations of the human spirit. He realised also that all religious assertions, revelations and dogmas had to be understood as ordered patternings of that boundless paradoxical background which he called the collective unconscious. In consequence, they can be researched and interpreted, explained and understood, and, like everything else the creative background produces, they belong to the unitary reality of the empirical world. It was of the deepest significance for Jung that this incorporation of religious contents still left the real secret of religion, its meta-physical origin, inviolate.

The fact that in this way Jung bridged over the gulf between science and religion, that he created a basis for a unitary world picture of which religious truths, till then excluded from it as objects of faith, form an integral part, may well be considered his most important contribution to the history of the mind. Only this unitary view can help to heal human suffering, for man has need of a living religion. And where the approach to genuine faith can no longer be found, a way is now opened that leads us on through experience and knowledge.

# 12

## THE INDIVIDUAL

Jung has disclosed and interpreted what is brewing in the unconscious of modern man and what must be done to palliate his suffering. His primary concern was individuation with its attendant experience of religious reality. This most subjective and most intimate of all experiences is not restricted to the personal but performs a function in collective life; it acts as a bulwark against the mounting flood of mass-mindedness that threatens us today. "The individual who is not anchored in God can offer no resistance on his own resources to the physical and moral blandishments of the world. For this he needs the evidence of an inner, transcendent experience which alone can protect him from the otherwise inevitable submersion in the mass."[1] Of collective significance, too, is the fact that increase of consciousness forces us to withdraw the projection of what we are unconscious of in ourselves—generally our own shadow-side—upon others, thus laying a solid foundation of relationship in the life of the individual and the community as well as in the life of nations.

But although the danger of submersion in the mass is obvious enough and is discussed on all sides, little attention is paid to the other, more subtle danger of identifying the ego with the contents of the unconscious—the danger of inflation. The identification of the ego with the archetype of the "Great Man" (the self), a veritable superman mania, is more of a danger today than ever, for superhuman powers of destruction have been given into man's hand. He possesses the weapon that could destroy all life on earth and is now setting out to conquer space. In the name of technology and progress he has upset the balance of nature on land and water, in the animal and plant world, and already there are schemes to produce any human types we please by computerised alterations of the genetic structure. The universal spread of the industrial-military power-complex with its diabolical plans for the future continues, with unremitting vehemence. Technological research, penetrating ever deeper into the secrets of the cosmos while leaving the results to be exploited for power purposes, cannot be held in check though this has more than once been demanded by responsible scientists. It springs from an irresistible spiritual impetus that is the privilege of the human species yet is directed almost exclusively to conquest and erosion of the external world. Because a corresponding exploration of the inner world through a deepening of consciousness and self-knowledge is disregarded, the balance between the two has been fatally disturbed. The dangers of unleashing a world cataclysm loom threateningly on the horizon and fear has become an ever more pervasive symptom. "The thread by which our fate hangs is wearing thin. Not nature, but the 'genius of mankind', has knotted the hangman's noose with which it can execute itself at any moment."[2] For all our affluence and know-how, everyone feels insecure and hounded by the nemesis of power.

The way to restore the balance and to guard against inflation and "superman mania" is the unspectacular way of individuation. It is a hard way—in Jung's sceptical eyes it is far more difficult to follow it and to find oneself than to make a landing on Mars. Yet more than ever depends on conscious individuality, for history and political change are played out not only as collective events but have their origin in the individual. "The whole future, the whole history of the world, ultimately spring as a gigantic summation from these hidden sources in individuals. In our most private and most subjective lives we are not only the passive witnesses of our age, and its sufferers, but also its makers."[3] Without the individual there is no community, and without community "even the free and self-secured individual cannot in the long run prosper".[4] But the unconscious man, who knows nothing of his destiny and his obligation to fulfil it, runs the risk of losing his personality in the mass. As a particle in the mass he is incapable of self-reliance and without any sense of individual responsibility, for which we have terrifying examples both past and present.

The individual is the source of historical change and the vehicle of social life, just as he is the source and vehicle of religious transformations. Collectivities in the biological, social and political sphere are made up of individuals; it is they who give them form, and "only in the individual can life fulfil its meaning".[5] For this reason Jung's psychotherapeutic and paedogogic interests were directed exclusively to individuals, and the danger of their perishing in the mass or being destroyed by inflation worried him deeply. "I am neither spurred on by excessive optimism nor in love with high ideals, but am merely concerned with the fate of the individual human being—that infinitesimal unit on whom the fate of the world depends, and in whom, if we read the meaning of the Christian message aright, even God seeks his goal."[6]

The significance of the individual is also being stressed by theology today, and here as well the prime reason is to counter-act the menacing collectivisation of the world and the Church and to preserve Christianity as a living force. Again it is Paul Tillich who comes closest to Jung's thought when he pleads respect for the individual human being as a vessel of the spirit and demands that his religious "maturity" (Bonhoeffer) be

taken seriously. The Church must, he says, pay serious attention to the religious experiences of individuals and cherish
them.[7] That is why he calls for a "prophetic Protestantism"
which is "necessary for every Church and for every secular
movement if it is to avoid disintegration".[8] Tillich sees in this
"protestant" way out of the present crisis of the Church a
working of the Holy Ghost—a "prophetic spirit which bloweth
where it listeth, without ecclesiastical regulations, organisations
and traditions".[9]

There is, nevertheless, a difference of principle between
Tillich's views and Jung's: Tillich is prepared to throw tradition overboard. For Jung tradition was the spiritual bedrock
for all future development whether collective or individual.
The new can bear fruit only when it grows from seeds im-
planted in tradition.[10] The man with roots in the unconscious
is also rooted in the archetypal images tradition has handed
down to him. Separation from the historical man in him can
never be complete and final. That is why Jung never swerved
from the Judaeo-Christian tradition but observed and interpreted it through the eyes of a modern man trained in the
natural and social sciences. Future generations will, if the
spirit retains its vitality, offer yet other interpretations and
continue the tradition in their own way and with new
knowledge

A "prophetic Protestantism" in Tillich's sense can hardly be
denied in Jung. Whether it will be heard and will take effect
only the future will show. He himself, with that sober and
impersonal sense of values that was peculiar to him, spoke
more than once of the posthumous significance of his work.

# 13

## MEANING AS THE MYTH
## OF CONSCIOUSNESS

*Creative Consciousness*

The deeper Jung penetrated into the laws of archetypal processes underlying the manifestations of the unconscious, the more essential the role of consciousness seemed to him. Consciousness was already well developed in the animal kingdom. Man possesses a consciousness that not only perceives and reacts to what it experiences, but is aware of perceiving and understands what it is experiencing. It has the faculty of reflexion[1] and insight, and, through its recognition of the outer and inner world, of self-extension and self-transformation. Man's consciousness is also a spiritual function. It lifts him out of the animal kingdom, even though from another point of view he can be regarded as a differentiated animal driven by instinct.[2] Generally Jung used "consciousness" and "reflecting consciousness" as equivalent concepts, occasionally substituting "mind", and "man" as the vehicle of mind. The cognising and reflecting consciousness exercises a creative activity, superimposing on the existence of the outer and inner world the fact that they are *known*. In this way it endows them with reality: "the world becomes the phenomenal world", and as though in a "second cosmogony" man confirms its existence for the Creator.[3]

When, from a low hill in the Athi plains of East Africa, Jung gazed into the wide savannah and watched the vast herds of

gazelle, antelope, gnu, zebra and warthog in the soundless stillness, he had as it were a primeval experience of the creative
function of consciousness.[4] Thirty years later he recapitulated
it in his memoirs: "Grazing, heads nodding, the herds moved
forward like slow rivers. There was scarcely any sound save the
melancholy cry of a bird of prey. This was the stillness of the
eternal beginning, the world as it had always been, in the state
of non-being; for until then no one had been present to know
that it was this world . . . There the cosmic meaning of consciousness became overwhelmingly clear to me . . . Man is
indispensable for the completion of creation; he himself is the
second creator of the world, who alone has given to the world
its objective existence—without which, unheard, unseen,
silently eating, giving birth, dying, heads nodding through
hundreds of millions of years, it would have gone on in the
profoundest night of non-being down to its unknown end.
Human consciousness created objective existence and meaning,
and man found his indispensable place in the great process of
being."[5]

Man has an indispensable place in the spiritual world too,
with its age-long processes of transformation. His consciousness, as we have seen, plays a creative part in the evolution and
differentiation of archetypal God-images. We might say that
he accomplishes the miracle of a second theogony. As co-
creator of outer and inner reality he and his consciousness have
a "cosmic responsibility".[6] Jung even speaks of the "miracle
of reflecting consciousness"[7] in which the whole evolutionary
trend of nature culminates. "The importance of consciousness
is so great that one cannot help suspecting the element of
*meaning* to be concealed somewhere within all the monstrous,
apparently senseless biological turmoil, and that the road to
its manifestation was ultimately found on the level of warm-
blooded vertebrates possessed of a differentiated brain—found

as if by chance, unintended and unforeseen, and yet somehow sensed, felt and groped for out of some dark urge."[8]

The same thought occurs in Meister Eckhart: "The innermost nature of all grain is wheat, of all metal gold, of all birth man",[9] and in Thomas Mann: "In my deepest soul I hug the supposition that with God's 'Let there be', which summoned the cosmos out of nothing, and with the generation of life from the inorganic, it was man who was ultimately intended, and that with him a great experiment is initiated, the failure of which because of man's guilt would be the failure of creation itself, amounting to its refutation. Whether that be so or not, it would be well for man to behave as if it were so."[10]

Jung's myth of meaning is the myth of consciousness. The metaphysical task of man resides in the continual expansion of consciousness at large, and his destiny as an individual in the creation of individual self-awareness. It is consciousness that gives the world a meaning. "Without the reflecting consciousness of man the world is a gigantic meaningless machine, for as far as we know man is the only creature that can discover 'meaning'," Jung wrote to Erich Neumann (March 1959). And to a young woman struck by heavy blows of fate he wrote in June 1956: "The boon of increased self-awareness is the sufficient answer even to life's suffering", otherwise it would be meaningless and unendurable. "Though the suffering of creation which God left imperfect cannot be done away with by the revelation of the good God's will to man, yet it can be mitigated and made meaningful."

However, Jung's emphasis on consciousness was never intended as a devaluation of the unconscious, nor did he ever imagine it could be "conquered". A replacement of the unconscious by consciousness is altogether unthinkable considering that the scope of the two cannot be compared, and that consciousness acquires its creative power only through being rooted in the unconscious even though we may be totally unaware of its existence. Jung's high estimate of consciousness was present in the germ from the very beginning, but he came to recognise its paramount role in human destiny only in the course of the years. To begin with he trusted the creative powers of the unconscious, as he had not yet plumbed the depths of its paradoxical nature. It was this that misled him to give the beginnings of National Socialism a chance in spite of all his objective reservations. He saw it, quite correctly, as an eruption of collective forces from the unconscious, but was still inclined at the time to give the myth of the unconscious precedence over the myth of consciousness.[11]

His basic thoughts about the myth of consciousness and its meaning may be found in his memoirs. This is no accident, as he considered the book not a scientific work and the answer to the question of meaning not a scientific answer. Every answer is a human interpretation or conjecture, a confession or a belief.[12] It is created by consciousness, and its formulation is a myth.

Jung created his answer on the basis of insights he had gained through long years of research work. In a short passage in the memoirs he once more described how the ambivalence of the Old Testament God-image leads to the "myth of the necessary incarnation of God" and finally to the synthesising experience of the self: "The necessary internal contradictions in the image of a Creator-god can be reconciled in the unity and wholeness of the self . . . In the experience of the self it is no longer the 'God' and 'man' that are reconciled, as it was before, but rather the opposites within the God-image itself. That is the meaning of 'divine service', the service which man can render to God, that light may emerge from the darkness, that the Creator may become conscious of his creation, and man conscious of himself.

"That is the goal, or one goal, which fits man meaningfully into the scheme of creation, and at the same time confers meaning upon it. It is an explanatory myth which has slowly taken shape within me in the course of the decades. It is a goal I can acknowledge and esteem, and which therefore satisfies me."[13]

Its limitation to a subjective statement detracts nothing from Jung's "explanatory myth". It gradually crystallised out of a knowledge of man and his psyche that went deeper than most knowledge in our time, and it is a meaningful continuation of the two-thousand-year-old Judaeo-Christian myth. Hence it applies not to Jung only, but has a significance that extends beyond the personal. Jung was aware of this, for he goes on: "I do not imagine that in my reflections on the meaning of man and his myth I have uttered a final truth, but I think that this is what can be said at the end of our aeon of the Fishes, and perhaps must be said in view of the coming aeon of Aquarius (the Water Bearer), who has a human figure."[14] Jung wrote these words in his eighty-fourth year, gazing into a distant future. One may well conclude that at the end of his life he had the feeling of having discharged the "cosmic responsibility" of man to the best of his ability, and of having fulfilled the task of broadening consciousness which was laid upon him as it is upon every one of us. In the memoirs, the chapter on his work ends with the words: "I have the feeling that I have done all that it was possible for me to do. Without a doubt that life-work could have been larger, and could have been done better; but more was not within my power."[15]

When Erich Neumann read the draft of the last chapter of the memoirs, which contains Jung's late thoughts on meaning, in 1958, he wrote him a letter expressing his general agreement while demurring on certain points. The crucial passages are as follows: "Precisely because the psyche and the archetypes with their meaning evolved in the course of natural evolution, their meaning is not something alien to nature but pertains to it from the very outset—so it seems to me . . . This is the only thing that remains questionable: What is creation for? The answer, that what shines only in itself when unreflected may shine in infinite variety, is age-old, but satisfies me."

Jung saw meaning in the reciprocal relationship between man's deepening self-awareness and an unfolding of the God-image (metaphorically formulated as "God's consciousness of himself"); for Neumann there was no such retroaction on God nor did there need to be one. Jung's answer (March 1959) gives us once again the rationale of his standpoint or confession. The mode of address "Dear Friend", which he used but rarely, is an indication of the intimacy that had grown up between them in their endeavour to understand each other's cast of mind. The letter reads in part: "Since a creation without the reflecting consciousness of man has no *discernible* meaning, the hypothesis of a *latent* meaning endows man with cosmogonic significance, a true *raison d'être*. If on the other hand the latent meaning is ascribed to the Creator as a conscious plan of creation, the question arises: Why should the creator stage-manage this whole world phenomenon since he already knows what he can reflect himself in, and why should he reflect himself at all since he is already conscious of himself? Why should he create alongside his own omniscience a second, inferior consciousness—millions of dreary little mirrors when he knows in advance just what the image they reflect will look like?"[16]

Shortly afterwards, Jung wrote much the same thing in a letter to Miguel de Serrano (September 1960): "(The light of consciousness) is most precious not only to me, but above all to the darkness of the creator, who needs man to illuminate his creation. If God had foreseen his world, it would be a mere

K

senseless machine and man's existence a useless freak. My intellect can envisage the latter possibility, but the whole of my being says 'No' to it."[17]

The value Jung set on *prayer* arises from this religious intuition, permeated with feeling, of a meaningful I-Thou relationship between man and God. He says in a letter (September 1943): "I have thought much about prayer. It—prayer—is very necessary because it makes the Beyond we conjecture and think about an immediate reality, and transposes us into the duality of the ego and the dark Other. One hears oneself speaking and can no longer deny that one has addressed 'That'. The question then arises: What will become of Thee and of Me? of the transcendental Thou and the immanent I? The way of the unexpected opens, fearful and unavoidable, with hope of a propitious turn or a defiant 'I will not perish under the will of God unless I myself will it too'. Then only, so I feel, is God's will made perfect. Without me it is only his almighty will, a frightful fatality even in its grace, void of sight and hearing, void of knowledge for precisely that reason. I go together with it, an immensely weighty milligram without which God had made his world in vain . . .''

Jung's avowal of a creator who needs man just as much as man needs him projects an image that is well-known in mysticism and philosophy and occurs also in modern poetry.[18] Jung himself was fond of quoting the *Cherubinischer Wandersmann* of Angelus Silesius (Johannes Scheffler, 1624–77). In *Psychological Types*[19] he cites these verses among others:

I know that without me
God can no moment live.
Were I to die, then he
No longer could survive.

> To illuminate my God
> The sunshine I must be.
> My beams must radiate
> His vast unpainted sea.

Meister Eckhart, to whose mind and work Jung felt particularly drawn, should also be mentioned in this connection.
His saying: "I am the cause that God is God!"[20] reflects a
similar view of the God-man relationship. Nor should we
forget Hegel (1770–1831), where we find such formulations as
"Without the world God is not God" and "God is God only
in so far as he knows himself; moreover his self-knowledge is
his consciousness of himself in man and man's knowledge *of*
God."[21] At the turn of the century Rilke clothed this thought
in poetic form:[22]

> What will you do, God, should I die?
> Should your cup break? That cup am I.
> Your drink go bad? That drink am I.
> I am the trade you carry on,
> With me is all your meaning gone.

The correspondence exchanged between Jung and Neumann
about God and man makes impressive but difficult reading:
two psychotherapists, teacher and pupil, Christian and Jew,
both wrestling a few years before their death with the question
of meaning, neither of them hesitating to avow a faith founded
in each case on hard mental work, research and profound
experience. Jung's God, evolving and taking shape through his
encounter with man, is a primordial image. Neumann's God,
abiding in immutable repose, is another primordial image,
equally profound and significant. They correspond to the flux
and change, genesis and decay of Heraclitus, and the self-
subsistent, unchanging One of Parmenides. As Jung himself

says: "After all, we can imagine God as an eternally flowing current of vital energy that endlessly changes shape just as easily as we can imagine him as an eternally unmoved, unchangeable essence."[23] Neither the one nor the other image tells us anything about God himself. The significant and exciting thing is the fact that Jung, like Neumann, took the step from knowledge of the archetypal foundations of such images to the mythic statement, to faith and the asseveration of meaning. For neither of them did this decision amount to a denial of the psychological foundation of mythic statements, but both preserved the freedom to create a myth of meaning.

One naturally asks oneself whether a "man-made" meaning is of any value, and whether the impossibility of discovering an objective meaning would not be better answered with an admission of meaninglessness. Jung answered no to this question. His denial was not only the expression of a deeply religious temperament but also the outcome of his experience as a psychotherapist and a doctor: "Meaninglessness inhibits fullness of life and is therefore equivalent to illness."[24] He saw psychoneurosis as, "ultimately, the suffering of a soul which has not discovered its meaning",[25] whereas meaning has an inherent curative power: "Meaning makes a great many things endurable—perhaps everything."[26] A universally valid formula for meaning does not exist, and up to the end of his life Jung allotted a place for both meaning and meaninglessness in his scheme of things. Yet the creation of meaning is important in so far as the "meaningful divides itself from the meaningless. When sense and nonsense are no longer identical, the force of chaos is weakened by their subtraction; sense is then endued with the force of meaning, and nonsense with the force of meaninglessness. In this way a new cosmos arises."[27]

In comparison with this view of the world, the dark vision

of poets and writers of our century, proclaiming meaninglessness and consequent despair to be the inner truth of man, is
tragically one-sided. The fact that the literature of the
"absurd", of nihilism and despair occupies so broad a place is
symptomatic of an age that has lost its religious roots and
cannot look the paradox of a transcendental reality in the eye.
The most important of these works leaves us in no doubt that
it is man who has failed. They paint a picture of the man who,
from feebleness and ineptitude, has not won through to a
meaning and cannot win through to it, because though he
may divine it he does not create it. Two names come to mind.

In Franz Kafka (1883-1924), who was the first to give valid
artistic expression to the metaphysical plight of modern man,
the experience of meaninglessness is condensed in the parable
of the man who spends his whole life seeking in vain for
"admittance to the Law". For days and years he sits at the side
of the half-open "door of the Law", waiting for the powerful
door-keeper to let him enter. He wastes his whole life sense-
lessly waiting in monotonous despair. Finally his eyes grow
dim and the world darkens around him. "But in the darkness
he can now perceive a radiance that streams immortally from
the door of the Law." The dying man asks the door-keeper why
in all these years no one but him has come seeking admittance,
since everyone strives to attain the Law. Whereupon the door-
keeper bellows in his ear: "No one but you could gain admittance through this door, since this door was intended only for
you. I am now going to shut it."[28]

Of living contemporary writers we will mention only
Samuel Beckett (b. 1906) as the apostle of tragic meaninglessness. In all his books nothing, fundamentally, happens, everything moves round in an endless circle and the everlasting litany
of meaninglessness begins again, because man does not see the
essential, or seeing it does not understand; because he does not

create meaning but waits for it and so ends in never-ending disappointment.

Life offers no interpretation, and to that extent it appears meaningless. But it has a nature that can be interpreted, that the discriminating intellect can discern, "for in all chaos there is a cosmos, in all disorder a secret order, in all caprice a fixed law, for everything that works is grounded on its opposite".[29] An unequivocal "No" to the question of meaning does not comprehend the whole, which is always a paradox. The opposite is lacking, the "Yes". That is why the question goes on living as always, and confronts man over and over again; for "meaning" is an archetype,[30] just as the riddle of existence and "intimations of immortality" are archetypal experiences.

### The Secret of Simplicity

Every statement about meaning, whether it be an hypothesis or a confession of faith, is a myth, a product partly of consciousness and partly of the unconscious. But modern man is too rational, too smart, too much of a know-all, too far removed from nature and her contradictions to take his own intimations or the images arising from his psyche seriously. He has forgotten how to create myths, and because of this he has failed to go on building the Christian myth. This was the gravamen of Jung's "protest" against contemporary Christianity. He himself applied his research to the task of understanding the Bible and dogma anew through the psychology of the unconscious. The old truths were clothed in the garment of a new yet immemorial myth which, conjoined to the God-image of the Holy Ghost, draws the ordinary sinful man into the divine drama. That is why the myth concerns him in a very special way. For Jung it became an experience of meaning.

Because the primitive is so close to nature, the meaning of his myths gives him a sense of security. Everything he does, everything he experiences, is intimately connected with the cosmos, with the stars and the wind, with sacred animals and gods. Modern man, with his incomparably more differentiated consciousness, has lost touch with nature both without and within, with his psychic images and therefore with meaning. He is one-sided, and he goes on developing one-sidedly along the path of intellectual differentiation. The primitive child of nature, who yet dwells within him, was repressed, consequently it degenerated and from time to time goes berserk and turns him into a pitiless barbarian. Contact with the unconscious, which heals and makes whole, restores the connection with his origin, with the source of psychic images. This is not a reversion to barbarism, but regeneration through a renewed and conscious relationship with a living spirit buried in the unconscious. Every step forward on the way to individuation is at the same time a step backwards into the past, into the mysteries of one's own nature.[31]

When Jung, in his eighties, was discussing at his house the process of becoming conscious with a group of young psychiatrists from America, England and Switzerland, he ended with the surprising words: "And then you have to learn to become decently unconscious." This was not a disavowal of his own work, nor a depreciation of consciousness, but a hint that every attempt at greater consciousness is followed, or should be followed, by an enantiodromia into unconsciousness. Yet unconsciousness at the end of the process is of a different kind from the unconsciousness at its beginning, just as a mountain seen from the valley looks different after one has climbed it. With this "unconsciousness of consciousness" scientific observation reaches its bourn. It is the beginning of the way — no longer definable by the intellect — to meaning and wisdom.

Those who have experienced the archetype of meaning, or have created a myth of meaning or made it their own, need no longer interpret. They know: "It is". The ephemeral surface of life is no longer a veil hiding the transcendental reality, for both worlds now coalesce in a meaningful unity. Then the meaning of the wind is simply the wind, of love, love, of life, life. What at the beginning of the way was sheer unconscious-ness and emptiness, or appeared commonplace, now contains the secret of simplicity in which the opposites are united.

When one does "the next and most necessary thing without fuss and with conviction, one is always doing something meaningful and intended by fate".[32] So Jung once described simplicity in daily life. "But simple things are always the most difficult" is the corollary that recurs in many places in his work.[33] Simplicity is a great art, because it is in constant danger of being wrecked in collision with the world or by unconsciousness, but it remains a goal. It brings that original, transcendental wholeness of the self into reality once its opposites become conscious and its multitudinous aspects are made one again.

### Synchronicity

It is man who creates meaning. Yet, given a view of the world that includes the unconscious, this statement too must be com-plemented by its opposite: the hypothesis of a meaning subsist-ing in itself and independent of man.

An *a priori* meaning seems to manifest itself chiefly in phenomena that Jung described as "synchronistic". These include, for instance, extrasensory perceptions: dreams that come true, verifiable premonitions, genuine foreknowledge, etc. All such phenomena are characterised by the fact that an inner psychic image (dream, vision, precognition) mirrors a future or distant external event inaccessible to the organs of sense. Both the inner experience and the outer event are con-nected with one another not causally but by the equivalence of their content, by the element of *meaning*. In other cases the event happening in reality meaningfully repeats or supplements the inner experience: for instance a rose-chafer, which is related to the scarab, flies against the window at the very moment when a patient is telling the analyst her dream of a golden scarab.[34] Or else an acquaintance appears round the corner just when one is thinking of him, or a clock stops at the moment of a person's death, and so on. With these and similar border-line phenomena, occurring irregularly and relatively infrequently,[35] two or more independent events each possessing its own causal chain are connected with one another by meaning. Their connection cannot be explained causally, for which reason Jung introduced the new concept of *synchronicity* as a necessary principle of knowledge. He defined it as a "coincidence in time of two or more causally unrelated events which have the same or a similar meaning";[36] it "could be added as a fourth to the recognised triad of space, time, and causality".[37] The "coincidence in time" does not refer to an absolute simultaneity determined by the clock, though such a thing can also happen. It is rather a question of the subjective experience or inner image through which the past or future real event is experienced in the present. Image and event coincide in a subjective simultaneity. Because of this Jung preferred the terms "synchronicity" and "synchronistic" to "synchronism" and "synchronous".[38]

Synchronistic phenomena, and especially acausal extrasensory perceptions, led Jung to infer the existence of a transcendental meaning independent of consciousness. "The 'absolute knowledge' which is characteristic of synchronistic phenomena, a knowledge not mediated by the senses, supports the hypothesis of a self-subsistent meaning, or even expresses its existence. Such a form of existence can only be transcendental."[39]

With regard to our question of meaning it is of paramount

significance that this conception of it gradually took second place in the course of Jung's pioneer work on synchronicity. The concept of *pre-existent meaning* as characteristic of such phenomena was gradually replaced by the more objective concept of *acausal orderedness*.[40] The archetype, the structural element in the collective unconscious, must be considered the ordering factor. Experience has shown that synchronistic phenomena are most likely to occur in the vicinity of archetypal happenings like death, deadly danger, catastrophes, crises, upheavals, etc. One could also say that in the unexpected parallelism of psychic and physical happenings, which characterises these phenomena, the paradoxical, psychoid archetype has "ordered" itself: it appears here as a psychic image, there as a physical, material, external fact. Since we know that the conscious process consists in the perception of opposites which throw each other into relief, a synchronistic phenomenon could be understood as an unusual way of becoming conscious of an archetype. Part of the archetype is still in the unconscious, hence the relativity of space and time characteristic of processes outside or beyond consciousness. But another part of it has broken through into consciousness, hence its originally unknowable psychoid unity splits into opposites that can now be recognised, into psychic and physical parallel events.

Seen from the standpoint of the more comprehensive conception of acausal orderedness, synchronicity is only a special instance of a general orderedness, which holds good in the sciences as well and embraces outside and inside, cosmos and mind, knower and known. The concept of "meaning" remains just as characteristic of synchronistic phenomena as before, but it now takes on once more the quality of something created by man: the orderedness that comes to light in acausal events can be experienced as meaningful, or else dismissed as pure chance and therefore meaningless.

In the majority of cases an experience of the hidden, transcendental, ordering factor is bound up with an awareness of numinosity. This is true of the physical sciences, which, having reached the frontiers of cognition, find themselves faced with metaphysical and religious questions. It is equally true of psychology, now that it has established the numinous effects of the archetype. The synchronistic phenomena arranged by the archetype often arouse wonder and awe, or an intuition of unfathomable powers which assign meaning. In Goethe's view there exists an ordering power outside man, which resembles chance as much as providence, and which contracts time and expands space. He called it the "daemonic", and spoke of it as others speak of God.[41]

Causalism breaks everything down into discrete processes, and this is absolutely necessary if we are to gain reliable knowledge of the world. But the principle of synchronicity, taking into account the psychoid archetype and a cosmic order to which "both the psyche of the perceiver and that which is recognised in the perception are subject",[42] allows us to glimpse, behind the discrete processes, a universal interrelationship of events. A pre-existent unity of being takes shape, and the seemingly incommensurable worlds of physis and psyche can be understood as aspects of this unity.

Today, in an age increasingly rent by spiritual fragmentation, such a conception has an important role to play in compensating our picture of the world. This unitary vision of reality is a scientific analogue of the religious experience of an archetypal God-image in which the opposites are reconciled. Jung rediscovered it in the unconscious of modern man, as the image of wholeness. In raising it to consciousness and thus actualising it, he saw, or created for himself, the meaning of life.

# Notes

# Notes

### *Foreword*

1. Revised and expanded as "A Psychological Approach to the Dogma of the Trinity," in *Psychology and Religion: West and East.*

2. Princeton University Press, Bollingen Series, Princeton 1973 and Routledge & Kegan Paul, London, 1973.

### *1. The Theme*

1. *The Archetypes and the Collective Unconscious*, par. 65.

2. *Memories, Dreams, Reflections.* Recorded and edited by Aniela Jaffé, (trans. Richard and Clara Winston) pp. 358 f. (p. 330). (The pagination of the British edition, which differs from that of the American, is given throughout in brackets.)

3. Contained in *Psychology and Religion.*

4. "Psychotherapists or the Clergy", *ibid.*, par. 497. See also Gerhard Adler, "Die Sinnfrage in der Psychotherapie", in *Psychotherapeutische Probleme;* Fierz, "Sinn im Wahn", in *Klinik und analytische Psychologie;* Neumann, "Die Sinnfrage und das Individuum", *Eranos-Jahrbuch 1957.*

5. "The Aims of Psychotherapy", in *The Practice of Psychotherapy*, par. 83.

6. "Psychotherapists or the Clergy", par. 516.     7. *Ibid.*, par. 509.

8. "Analytical Psychology and *Weltanschauung*", in *The Structure and Dynamics of the Psyche*, par. 739.

9. "Spirit and Life", *ibid.*, par. 647.

### *2. The Unconscious and the Archetype*

1. Lancelot L. Whyte, in his book *The Unconscious before Freud*, discusses the concept of the unconscious in Shakespeare, Leibniz, Goethe, Schopenhauer, Nietzsche, V. Hartmann and others. A philosophical concept analogous to that of the unconscious can be found in antiquity, above all in Plotinus (A.D. 205-70).

2. "Medicine and Psychotherapy", in *The Practice of Psychotherapy*, par. 204.

3. Cf. Jung, "The Psychology of the Transference", *ibid.*, par. 356,

n. 12: "I call unconscious processes 'hypothetical' because the unconscious is by definition not amenable to direct observation and can only be inferred."

4. "Concerning the Archetypes, with Special Reference to the Anima Concept", in *The Archetypes and the Collective Unconscious*, par. 118.

5. A thorough exposition of the archetype concept may be found in Jacobi, *Complex/Archetype/Symbol*, pp. 31 ff.

6. Cf. Kerényi, *Umgang mit Göttlichem*, p. 53. The oldest known literary passage in which the Greek word *archetypos* occurs is in Cicero (106-43 B.C.). In his letters to Atticus he translated it into Latin, thus giving it currency in late antiquity.

7. *Two Essays on Analytical Psychology*, par. 109. This early formulation does not make it clear that by "primordial images" Jung meant irrepresentable structural forms in the unconscious.

8. "The Influence of Archetypal Ideas on the Scientific Theories of Kepler", in *The Interpretation of Nature and the Psyche*, p. 153.

9. "Psychological Aspects of the Mother Archetype", in *The Archetypes and the Collective Unconscious*, par. 149.

10. *Ibid.*, par. 154.

11. In "Instinct and the Unconscious", in *The Structure and Dynamics of the Psyche*, par. 270.

12. Borrowed from Jacob Burckhardt. Cf. *Symbols of Transformation*, par. 45 and n. 45.

13. "Mother Archetype", par. 155. Cf. also "Psychological Commentary on The Tibetan Book of the Dead," in *Psychology and Religion*, par. 845: The archetypes as such "have at first no specific content. Their specific content only appears in the course of the individual's life, when personal experience is taken up in precisely those forms."

14. "On Psychic Energy", in *Dynamics*, pars. 99 f.

15. Cf. *Two Essays*, par. 109: "I have often been asked where the archetypes or primordial images come from. It seems to me that their origin can only be explained by assuming them to be deposits of the constantly repeated experiences of humanity". Also "The Structure of the Psyche", in *Dynamics*, pars. 337, 339, and *Psychological Types*, Definition 26: "Image".

16. "On the Nature of the Psyche", in *Dynamics*, par. 412.

17. "Mother Archetype", par. 187.

18. See also *infra*, p. 30.

19. *The Archetypes and the Collective Unconscious*, par. 6, n. 9.

20. Cf. Weibel, "Modell und Wirklichkeit in der biologischen Forschung", *Neue Zürcher Zeitung*, Nr. 3809 (13 Sept. 1964): "The biologist can grasp inner processes only indirectly, through their effects on surface areas of the object that are accessible to him. For this reason he must *think* these effects with the help of models and theories."

21. "Instinct and the Unconscious", par. 268.

22. "On the Nature of the Psyche", par. 404.

23. "Schizophrenia", in *The Psychogenesis of Mental Disease*, par. 565.

24. *Ibid.:* "On closer investigation [universal myth-motifs] prove to be typical attitudes, modes of action—thought-processes and impulses which must be regarded as constituting the instinctive behaviour typical of the human species. The term I chose for this, namely 'archetype', therefore coincides with the biological concept of the 'pattern of behaviour'."

25. "On the Nature of the Psyche", par. 406.

26. Jung, Foreword to Harding, *Woman's Mysteries*, p. x.

27. "On the Nature of the Psyche", par. 405. The "numinous" denotes the overwhelming power of religious experience. Cf. Otto, *The Idea of the Holy*.

28. *The Archetypes and the Collective Unconscious*, par. 34.

29. Cf. "On the Nature of the Psyche", par. 414: "The archetype . . . as well as being an image in its own right, is at the same time a *dynamism* which makes itself felt in the numinosity and fascinating power of the archetypal image."

30. *The Archetypes and the Collective Unconscious*, par. 35.

31. *Ibid.*, par. 36.

32. "On the Nature of the Psyche", par. 405.

33. Cf. *ibid.*, par. 402: "Image and meaning are identical; and as the first takes shape, so the latter becomes clear."

34. Jung defines the self as the archetype of human wholeness. It is truly the transcendental "organiser" of the individual's life. The development of his personality from birth to death, his inner and outer experiences, are an unfolding and actualisation of the archetypal self in the unconscious. Jung also defined the self as "life's goal", because it is "the completest expression of that fateful combination we call individuality". (*Two Essays*, par. 404.) Concerning the self see also *infra*, pp. 42 f., 78 ff., 112 ff.

35. *Infra*, pp. 79 ff.      36. *Kepler*, p. 152.

37. *Science and the Common Understanding*, pp. 56 ff.

38. "Psychotherapy and a Philosophy of Life", in *The Practice of Psychotherapy*, par. 177.

39. "On the Nature of the Psyche", par. 439.

40. Foreword to Harding, *Woman's Mysteries*, p. x: "The archetype is metaphysical because it transcends consciousness."

41. Cf. *infra*, p. 32.

42. "On the Nature of the Psyche", par. 420.

43. "The Psychology of the Child Archetype", in *The Archetypes and the Collective Unconscious*, par. 291.

44. "On the Nature of the Psyche", par. 414.

L

*3. Jung's Method and Style*
1. "On the Nature of the Psyche", par. 402.
2. *Two Essays*, par. 200.        3. *Ibid.*
4. "Mother Archetype", par. 187.
5. Jordan, *Der Naturwissenschaftler vor der religiösen Frage*, p. 341. In a letter (1952) Jung wrote: "The language I speak must be ambiguous, must have two meanings in order to be fair to the dual aspect of the psyche's nature. I strive quite consciously and deliberately for ambiguity of expression, because it is superior to singleness of meaning and reflects the nature of life. My whole temperament inclines me to be very unequivocal indeed. That is not difficult, but it would be at the cost of truth. I purposely allow all the overtones and undertones to chime in, because they are there anyway while at the same time giving a fuller picture of reality. Clarity makes sense only in establishing facts, but not in interpreting them . . ." [This letter appears only in the original Swiss edition of *Memories, Dreams, Reflections*, p. 375—Trans.] Cf. also *Mysterium Coniunctionis*, par. 715: "Unequivocal statements can be made only in regard to immanent objects; transcendental ones can be expressed only by paradox." Moreover "Nicholas of Cusa, in his *De docta ignorantia*, regarded antinomial thought as the highest form of reasoning." ("Psychology of the Transference", in *The Practice of Psychotherapy*, par. 527, n. 9.)

*4. The Hidden Reality*
1. *Mitteilungen der Naturforschenden Gesellschaft Bern*. Neue Folge, Bd. XIV.
2. 'Psychological Aspects of the Mother Archetype", par. 155.
3. Portmann, *Biologie und Geist* (1957). Alverdes published his "Die Wirksamkeit von Archetypen in den Instinkthandlungen der Tiere", *Zoologischer Anzeiger* (Bd. 119, Heft 9/10) as early as 1937.
4. "Gestaltung und Lebensvorgang", *Eranos-Jahrbuch 1960*, p. 330.
5. "Das Lebendige als vorbereitete Beziehung", *Eranos-Jahrbuch 1955*, p. 504.
6. "Sinndeutung als biologisches Problem", *Eranos-Jahrbuch 1957*, pp. 500 ff.
7. "Freiheit und Bindung in biologischer Sicht", *Eranos-Jahrbuch 1962*, p. 443.
8. "Gestaltung als Lebensvorgang", *Eranos-Jahrbuch 1960*, p. 363.
9. *Der Mensch und die naturwissenschaftliche Erkenntnis*, p. 38.
10. *Kepler*, p. 152.    11. *Op. cit.*, p. 38.    12. Pauli, *op. cit.*, p. 153.
13. *Ibid.*, pp. 208 f.

14. Pauli, "Aspekte der Ideen vom Unbewussten", *Dialectica*, VIII: 4, p. 229.

15. The strange fact that it is "not found exclusively in the psychic sphere, but can occur just as much in circumstances that are not psychic" is due to what Jung calls its "transgressivity". Cf. "Synchronicity: An Acausal Connecting Principle", in *The Structure and Dynamics of the Psyche*, par. 964.

16. *Infra*, pp. 150 ff.

17. Pauli, in his paper on Kepler, takes the controversy between him and Robert Fludd (1574–1637), an alchemist and Rosicrucian, as illustrating the growing schism between the medieval religious, and the modern quantitative, conception of nature.

18. *The Universe and Dr Einstein*, p. 101.

19. *Ibid.*, p. 103. Cf. Coloss. 1:16: "For by him [the invisible God] were all things created that are in heaven and that are in earth, visible and invisible . . ."

20. Cited in F. Dessauer's foreword to Bavink, *Die Naturwissenschaft auf den Wege zur Religion*, p. 15.

21. Cited in Weizsäcker, *The History of Nature*, p. 162.

22. *Op. cit.*, p. 61, n. 1.

23. Cf. *Psychology and Religion*, pars. 10 ff; "Mother Archetype", par. 190.

24. Cf. Adler, "Die Sinnfrage in der Psychotherapie", in *Psychotherapeutische Probleme*, pp. 9 ff.

25. *Memories, Dreams, Reflections*, p. 336 (pp. 308 f.)

26. Cf. "On Psychic Energy", pars. 123 ff.

27. Jung used this word not in the primitive animistic but in the Goethean sense of "the daemonic". See *infra*, p. 153. Socrates, too, had his "daemon".

28. *Memories, Dreams, Reflections*, pp. 336 f. (p. 310). Cf. "Answer to Job", par. 757: "It is only through the psyche that we can establish that God acts upon us, but we are unable to distinguish whether these actions emanate from God or from the unconscious. We cannot tell whether God and the unconscious are two different entities. Both are borderline concepts for transcendental contents."

29. "The Undiscovered Self", in *Civilization in Transition*, par. 565.

30. "Mother Archetype", par. 150.

31. Jung always fought against the assertion that his psychology was a kind of philosophy. He understood philosophy as a discipline that operates with metaphysical statements and concepts, whereas psychology is first and foremost an empirical science based on the observation of facts and their interpretation. Even an hypostatised concept like the self is an empirical concept in this sense. Jung's epistemological premise, on which all his work

is founded, must however be regarded as a philosophical aspect of it.

32. *The Physicist's Conception of Nature*, p. 24.

33. *The History of Nature*, p. 63.

34. Jung, "On the Nature of the Psyche", par. 437. Cf. *Mysterium Coniunctionis*, par. 787: "That the world inside and outside ourselves rests on a transcendental background is as certain as our own existence, but it is equally certain that the direct perception of the archetypal world inside us is just as doubtfully correct as that of the physical world outside us."

35. "Psychological Commentary on The Tibetan Book of the Great Liberation", in *Psychology and Religion*, par. 769.

36. Weizsäcker, "Das Verhältnis der Quantenmechanik zur Philosophie Kants", *Zum Weltbild der Physik*, 7. Aufl. Stuttgart, 1958.

37. Heisenberg, *op. cit.*, p. 15.

38. Jung, *The Archetypes and the Collective Unconscious*, par. 6.

39. Jung, *Aion*, par. 355. Cf. Heisenberg, *op. cit.*, p. 24: "From the very start we are involved in an argument between nature and man in which science plays only a part, so that the common division of the world into subject and object, inner and outer world, body and soul, is no longer adequate and leads us into difficulties."

40. Cf. von Salis, "Geschichte als Prozess", in *Transparente Welt*, p. 60.

41. Cited in Zimmer, *Umsturz im Weltbild der Physik*, p. 374.

42. *Mysterium Coniunctionis*, par. 787.

43. Jung, "Answer to Job", par. 757: "Strictly speaking, the God-image does not coincide with the unconscious as such, but with a special content of it, namely the self. It is this archetype from which we can no longer distinguish the God-image empirically". Goethe, in his eighty-first year, said much the same thing to his friend F. v. Müller: "No organism quite corresponds to the idea underlying it; behind each one there is the higher idea. That is my God, that is the God we are all eternally seeking and hope to behold, but we can only divine him, not gaze on him." (*Goethes Gespräche ohne Gespräche mit Eckermann*, ed. v. Biedermann, p. 696.)

44. Par. 15.

45. *Ibid.*, par. 247: "I may define the 'self' as the totality of the conscious and unconscious psyche, but this totality transcends our vision . . . In so far as the unconscious exists it is not definable; its existence is a mere postulate and nothing whatever can be predicted as to its possible contents. The totality can only be experienced in its parts and then only in so far as these are contents of consciousness; but *qua* totality it necessarily transcends consciousness. Consequently the 'self' is a pure borderline concept similar to Kant's *Ding an sich*. True, it is a concept that grows steadily clearer with experience—as our dreams show—without, however, losing anything of its transcendence. Since we cannot possibly know the boundaries of some-

thing unknown to us, it follows that we are not in a position to set any bounds to the self."

46. "The Holy Men of India", in *Psychology and Religion*, par. 956.

47. Revised edition, 1960.    48. *Eranos-Jahrbuch 1960.*

49. *Major Trends*, p. 12.  50. *Eranos-Jahrbuch 1960*, p. 168.   51. *Ibid.*

52. *Psychology and Alchemy*, par. 2.   53. *Ibid.*, par. 20.

54. *The Courage to Be*, p. 180.   55. *Ibid.*

56. *Auf der Grenze*, p. 166.    57. Par. 555.

58. C. F. v. Weizsäcker observed to a gathering of psychotherapists in March 1965: "Jung has seen exactly what was so important to Plato, that these ideas are powers . . . those very powers without which we cannot understand anything at all, only *through* them can we understand something . . . Indeed, science itself is grounded on archetypes." Cited in *Psychotherapie und religiöse Erfahrung*, ed. W. Bitter, p. 37.

59. Cf. Speiser, "Die Platonische Lehre vom unbekannten Gott und die christliche Trinität", *Eranos-Jahrbuch 1940/41*, p. 29.

60. "Answer to Job", par. 556. Cf. *ibid.*, par. 749, n. 2: "Owing to the undervaluation of the psyche that prevails everywhere, every attempt at adequate psychological understanding is immediately suspected of psychologism. It is understandable that dogma must be protected from this danger. If, in physics, one seeks to explain the nature of light, nobody expects that as a result there will be no light. But in the case of psychology everybody believes that what it explains is explained away."

### 5. Inner Experience

1. Genuine chemistry did play a role in the *opus alchymicum*, but work in the laboratory was closely connected with *theoria* or "philosophising", thus allowing fantasy activity free play. Cf. *Psychology and Alchemy*, pars. 342 ff., 401 ff., and Eliade, *Schmiede und Alchemisten*.

2. Before Jung, Herbert Silberer had undertaken a psychological interpretation of alchemy in his book *Problems of Mysticism and Its Symbolism*, originally published 1914.

3. *Psychology and Alchemy*, par. 11.

4. *Ibid.* The formulation "archetype of the God-image" is not really correct. Since the archetype is unknowable it cannot be connected with the concept of an image. It would be truer to say "archetypal God-image".

5. *Ibid.*, par. 14.     6. *Ibid.*, par. 11.

7. *Two Essays on Analytical Psychology*, par. 403.

8. Written in English.

9. Cf. "The Spirit Mercurius", in *Alchemical Studies*, par. 301, n. 16.

10. Büttner, *Meister Eckeharts Schriften und Predigten*, III, p. 195.

11. Abell, *Gespräche mit berühmten Komponisten*, p. 67.

12. *Der Sinn der Heiligen Scheift*, p. 81.

13. *Report to Greco*. Translated from the German version, *Rechen-schaftsbericht vor El Greco, Kindheit und Jugend.*

14. *Psychology and Alchemy*, par. 13. The passage reads in full: "So long as religion is only faith and outward form, and the religious function is not experienced in our own souls, nothing of any importance has happened. It has yet to be understood that the *mysterium magnum* is not only an actuality but is first and foremost rooted in the human psyche. The man who does not know this from his own experience may be a most learned theologian, but he has no idea of religion and still less of education."

15. *Psychology and Religion*, par. 168.     16. *Ibid.*, par. 167.

17. *Memories, Dreams, Reflections*, pp. 36 ff. (pp. 48 ff.).

18. *Ibid.*, p. xi (p. 14).

19. "Brother Klaus", in *Psychology and Religion*, par. 480.

20. Neumann, "Dank an Jung", in *Der Psychologe*, VII: 7.

21. *Psychology and Religion*, par. 76.     22. See *infra*, pp. 76 ff.

23. See *Memories, Dreams, Reflections*, ch. VI.     24. Par. 756.

25. *The Politics of Experience and the Bird of Paradise*, p. 91.

26. *Ibid.*, p. 102.     27. P. 106.     28. P. 104.

29. P. 136.     30. P. 107.     31. P. 137.

32. *The Psychogenesis of Mental Disease.*

33. *Memories, Dreams, Reflections*, ch. VI.

34. *Ibid.*, pp. 124 ff. (pp. 125 ff.).

35. *The Politics of Experience*, p. 97.

36. *Psychology and Alchemy*, par. 438.

37. *Memories, Dreams, Reflections*, p. 129 (p. 129).

38. *Supra*, p. 55.

39. Cf. Jaffé, "Symbolism in the Visual Arts", in the symposium edited by Jung, *Man and his Symbols*. The short quotations that follow are mostly from that essay. Sources: Hess, *Dokumente zum Verständnis der modernen Malerei*; Haftmann, *Paul Klee, Wege bildnerischen Denkens*; Kandinsky, *Ueber das Geistige in der Kunst*; Read, *A Concise History of Modern Painting.*

40. Ch. VII: "The Type Problem in Aesthetics".

41. This is also true of the "pop art" we hear so much about today. According to one student of the subject, Allan Kaprow, the "simple concretism of pop" boils down to "quasi-realism". Pop is "light-hearted froth and a half-serious pointer to the continuing power of folk magic in our everyday lives". Cf. *Happenings*, ed. Becker and Vostell.

42. "Freud and Jung: Contrasts", in *Freud and Psychoanalysis*, par. 771.

43. *Ibid.*, par. 777.

44. *The Doors of Perception*, p. 15.     45. *Ibid.*     46. P. 12.     47. *Ibid.*

48. "Voraussetzung der Einweihung in Eleusis", in *Initiation*, ed. Blecker,

and "Mescalin-Perioden der Religionsgeschichte", in *Wege zum Menschen*, 17 Jhg., Heft 6, pp. 201 ff.—The drink consisted of barley, water, and the fresh leaves of *Menta pulegium* (pennyroyal). The effect of the slightly intoxicating but very innocuous drink was probably due to the nine-day fast that preceded initiation.

49. *My Self and I*, p. 46.

50. In "Schizophrenia" (*The Psychogenesis of Mental Disease*), par. 569, Jung explains the effect of mescalin as "a decay of apperception, such as can be observed in cases of extreme *abaissement du niveau mental* (Janet) and in intense fatigue and severe intoxication". Mescalin and kindred drugs "cause, as we know, an *abaissement* which, by lowering the threshold of consciousness, renders perceptible the perceptual variants that are normally unconscious, thereby enriching one's apperception to an astounding degree, but on the other hand making it impossible to integrate them into the general orientation of consciousness. This is because the accumulation of variants that have become conscious give each single act of apperception a dimension that fills the whole of consciousness. This explains the fascination so typical of mescalin."

51. Written in English.          52. Sorcerer's apprentice.

53. Letter to Ida Herz, 21 March 1954, in *Neue Rundschau*, 2.

54. Masters and Houston, *The Varieties of Psychedelic Experience*, p. 308.

### 6. Individuation

1. The fantasies of the alchemists could also be described as a species of active imagination. See *Psychology and Alchemy*, pars. 347 ff., 357, 390 ff. For the method of active imagination see "The Transcendent Function", in *The Structure and Dynamics of the Psyche*, pars. 167 ff., and *Mysterium Coniunctionis*, pars. 706, 753 f.

2. "Aims of Psychotherapy", in *The Practice of Psychotherapy*, par. 98.

3. "It is true that there are unprofitable, futile, morbid, and unsatisfying fantasies whose sterile nature is immediately recognised by every person endowed with common sense; but the faulty performance proves nothing against the normal performance." *Ibid.*

4. "The Transcendent Function", par. 189.

5. *Two Essays on Analytical Psychology*, par. 369.

6. "The Transcendent Function", par. 185.

7. "On the Nature of the Psyche", in *The Structure and Dynamics of the Psyche*, par. 402.

8. *Ibid.*, par. 400. For the concept of the individuation process see Jacobi, *The Way of Individuation*. Accounts of its practical aspect may be found in Jung, "A Study in the Process of Individuation", in *The Archetypes and the Collective Unconscious*, and Gerhard Adler, *The Living Symbol*.

9. "On the Nature of the Psyche", par. 402.
10. *Psychology and Alchemy*, par. 330.    11. *Ibid.*
12. "Answer to Job", in *Psychology and Religion*, par. 756.
13. "The Holy Men of India", in *ibid.*, par. 957 end.
14. *Psychology and Alchemy*, par. 330.
15. "Answer to Job", par. 745.
16. *Psychology and Alchemy*, par. 105. Cf. "Answer to Job", par. 756: "The difference between the 'natural' individuation process, which runs its course unconsciously, and the one which is consciously realised, is immense. In the first case consciousness nowhere intervenes; the end remains as dark as the beginning. In the second case so much darkness comes to light that the personality is permeated with light, and consciousness necessarily gains in scope and insight."
17. *Psychology and Religion*, par. 133 end.
18. Cf. "Answer to Job", par. 758: "That is to say, even the enlightened person remains what he is, and is never more than his own limited ego before the One who dwells within him, whose form has no knowable boundaries, who encompasses him on all sides, fathomless as the abysms of the earth and vast as the sky."
19. Cf. Katha Upanishad 4, 13 (*The Ten Principal Upanishads*, p. 34): "That Person in the heart, no bigger than a thumb, burning like flame without smoke, maker of past and future, the same today and tomorrow, that is Self."
20. Cf. Svetasvatara Upanishad 3, 20 (*The Thirteen Principal Upanishads*, p. 402).
21. *Two Essays on Analytical Psychology*, pars. 231-2.
22. Cf. "The Psychology of the Transference", in *The Practice of Psychotherapy*, par. 448: "Individuation has two principal aspects: in the first place it is an internal and subjective process of integration, and in the second it is an equally indispensable process of objective relationship. Neither can exist without the other although sometimes the one and sometimes the other predominates. This double aspect has two corresponding dangers. The first is the danger of the patient's using the opportunities for spiritual development arising out of the analysis of the unconscious as a pretext for evading the deeper human responsibilities, and for affecting a certain 'spirituality' which cannot stand up to moral criticism; the third is the danger that atavistic tendencies may gain the ascendancy and drag the relationship down to a primitive level."
23. Cf. "The Stages of Life", in *The Structure and Dynamics of the Psyche*, par. 771: "The serious problems of life are never fully solved. If ever they should appear to be so it is a sure sign that something has been lost. The meaning and purpose of a problem seem to lie not in its solution but in our

working at it incessantly. This alone preserves us from stultification and petrifaction."

24. Par. 400.  25. *Psychology and Alchemy*, par. 330.

26. *The Development of Personality*, par. 300. "Anyone with a vocation hears the voice of the ihner man: he is *called*." *Ibid.*

27. *Aion*, par. 116.  28. *Ibid.*

29. *Two Essays*, par. 404.  30. *Two Essays*, par. 266.

31. *Infra*, pp. 138 ff.

32. *Die neue Wirklichkeit*, p. 27.  33. *Ibid.*, p. 28.

34. Sartre, *Words* (trans. Irene Clephane), p. 142.

35. Jung, "Transformation Symbolism in the Mass", in *Psychology and Religion*, par. 391.

36. A Psychological Approach to the Dogma of the Trinity", in *ibid.*, par. 233.

37. *Ibid.*  38. Letter, June 1949.

39. Cf. "The Holy Men of India", par. 960: "(The ego) puts forward its claims peremptorily, and very often in overt or covert opposition to the needs of the evolving self. In reality, i.e., with few exceptions, the entelechy of the self consists in a succession of endless compromises, ego and self laboriously keeping the scales balanced if all is to go well."

40. "Mass", par. 390. "Becoming conscious means continual renunciation because it is an ever-deepening concentration." (Letter, August 1953).

41. "Mass", par. 390.  42. *Ibid.*, par. 400.

43. "Concerning Rebirth", in *The Archetypes and the Collective Unconscious*, par. 217.

44. Cf. "Transformation Symbolism in the Mass", par. 391.

45. Cf. *Aion*, par. 125: "(If anyone) voluntarily takes the burden of completeness on himself, he need not find it 'happening' to him against his will in a negative form. This is as much to say that anyone who is destined to descend into a deep pit had better set about it with all the necessary precautions rather than risk falling into the hole backwards."

46. *Markings*, p. 169.

47. The mathematician Hermann Weyl formulates the paradox of freedom in similar terms: "The mind is free within the bondage of its existence; its field is the possible, which is open to the infinite, unlike the self-enclosed being. Only when the freedom of the mind binds itself to law does the mind reconstructively understand the bondage of the world, and of its own existence in the world." From "Wissenschaft als symbolische Konstruktion", *Eranos-Jahrbudh 1948*, p. 381.

48. *Auf der Grenze*, pp. 100 f.  49. *Ibid.*  50. Act 3, Scene 2.

51. Erich Neumann speaks of a "philosophy of rootlessness" when the individual "expresses only himself as pure ego and knows nothing of his

connection with the self in which even as an ego he is rooted, from which he originates, from which he lives, and which is inextinguishably present as his own numinous core." From "Die Sinnfrage und das Individuum", *Eranos-Jahrbuch 1957*, p. 20.

52. "Transformation Symbolism in the Mass", par. 391.

53. These words, a Delphic oracle, are incised over the doorway of Jung's house in Küsnacht, near Zürich, and also on his family tomb.

### 7. Good and Evil

1. Cf. in particular "A Psychological Approach to the Dogma of the Trinity" and "Answer to Job" (in *Psychology and Religion*), and "The Undiscovered Self", "A Psychological View of Conscience", and "Good and Evil in Analytical Psychology" (in *Civilization in Transition*). Secondary Literature: Neumann, *Depth Psychology and a New Ethic*; Schärf, *Satan in the Old Testament*; Frey-Rohn, "Evil from the Psychological Point of View", in *Evil*.

2. Cf. "The Psychology of the Transference", par. 400, n. 60.

3. *Memories, Dreams, Reflections*, p. 170 (p. 165).

4. Luther's words as formulated in historical tradition are rather different: "Therefore I cannot and will not recant, because to act against conscience is neither safe nor sound. So help me God, Amen." Cited in Lilje, Martin Luther in *Selbstzeugnissen und Bilddokumenten*, p. 85. See also Schär, "A Protestant View of Conscience", in *Conscience*, pp. 113 f.

5. *Memories, Dreams, Reflections*, p. 345 (p. 318).

6. *Ibid.*—"I do not regard it for a moment as particularly meritorious morally for a person to avoid everything that is customarily considered a sin. Ethical value attaches only to those decisions which are reached in situations of supreme doubt." (Letter, January 1949.)

7. "A Psychological Approach to the Dogma of the Trinity", par. 267.

8. *Memories, Dreams, Reflections*, pp. 115 ff. and 122 ff. (pp. 116 ff. and 123 ff.).

9. *Psychology and Alchemy*, par. 36.

10. Cf. *Memories, Dreams, Reflections*, pp. 329 f. (p. 304): "Moral evaluation is always founded upon the apparent certitudes of a moral code which pretends to know precisely what is good and what evil. But once we know how uncertain the foundation is, ethical decision becomes a subjective, creative act. We can convince ourselves of its validity only *Deo concedente*— that is, there must be a spontaneous and decisive impulse on the part of the unconscious. Ethics itself, the decision between good and evil, is not affected by this impulse, only made more difficult for us. Nothing can spare us the torment of ethical decision. Nevertheless, harsh as it may sound, we must have the freedom in some circumstances to avoid the known moral good

and do what is considered to be evil, if our ethical decision so requires."

11. "A Psychological Approach to the Dogma of the Trinity", par. 292. The passage runs in full: "The ability to 'will otherwise' must, unfortunately, be real if ethics are to make any sense at all. Anyone who submits to the law from the start, or to what is generally expected, acts like the man in the parable who buried his talent in the earth. Individuation is an exceedingly difficult task: it always involves a conflict of duties, whose solution requires us to understand that our 'counter-will' is also an aspect of God's will."

12. *Ibid.*, par. 290.

13. The oldest codification of Jewish religious law, compiled in six "classes" about A.D. 200 on the basis of scholastic traditions.

14. Werblowsky, "The Concept of Conscience in Jewish Perspective", in *Conscience*, pp. 96 f.

15. Cf. Scholem, "Gut und Böse in der Kabbala", *Eranos-Jahrbuch 1961*, pp. 29 ff.

16. *Ibid.*, p. 67.                    17. *Werke, VI*, p. 644.

18. *Theosophische Fragen oder 177 Fragen von göttlicher Offenbarung, Werke*, VI, p. 597.

19. Cf. Weiss, *Die Gnosis Jakob Böhmes*. For the moral ambivalence of the divine figures and highest spiritual ideas in Oriental myths and religions see Eliade, "La Coincidentia Oppositorum et le mystère de la totalité", *Eranos-Jahrbuch 1959*, pp. 195 ff., and Watts, *The Two Hands of God*.

### 8. Answer to Job

1. From Rudin, *Psychotherapie und Religion*, p. 13.

2. "Answer to Job", in *Psychology and Religion*, par. 584.

3. *Ibid.*, par. 733.

4. *Ibid.*, par. 558. Cf. *Memories, Dreams, Reflections*, p. 340 (p. 313): "The Word of God comes to us, and we have no way of distinguishing whether and to what extent it is different from God. There is nothing about this Word that could not be considered known and human, except for the manner in which it confronts us spontaneously and places obligations upon us. It is not affected by the arbitrary operation of our own will".

5. Cf. "Answer to Job", par. 738, n. 1: "Psychologically the God-concept includes every idea of the ultimate, of the first and last, of the highest and lowest. The name makes no difference."

6. "A Psychological Approach to the Dogma of the Trinity", par. 291.

7. *Supra*, pp. 29 ff.                    8. *Religionsphilosophie*, p. 76.

9. *The Courage to Be*, p. 174 (modified). Tillich often uses "ground of being" and "being-itself" as circumlocutions for God. Cf. Tillich, "Das neue Sein als Zentralbegriff", *Eranos-Jahrbuch 1954*, pp. 262 f.

10. "Answer to Job", par. 567.

11. "A Psychological View of Conscience", par. 844.

12. Cf. *Memories, Dreams, Reflections*, p. 338 (p. 311): "The myth must ultimately take monotheism seriously and put aside its dualism, which, however much repudiated officially, has persisted until now and enthroned an eternal dark antagonist alongside the omnipotent Good. Room must be made within the system for the philosophical *complexio oppositorum* of Nicholas of Cusa and the moral ambivalence of Jacob Boehme; only thus can the One God be granted the wholeness and synthesis of opposites which should be His."

13. Cf. Rudin, "C. G. Jung und die Religion", *Orientierung*, Nr. 21 (28. Jhg.); "It must of course be admitted that Jung did not appreciate the scholastic doctrine of evil—the *privatio boni*—and therefore drew upon his own head Victor White's charge of having misunderstood it radically. A mere *privatio* seemed to Jung far too innocuous to express adequately the formidable power of evil which we experience often enough. But the *privatio boni* does not by any means imply a mere dilution of good, it affirms a catastrophic loss of that value which, as so-called 'transcendence', belongs to the very foundations of being. When the *bonum* is diminished there is a simultaneous and insupportable diminution of being—its completeness is destroyed."

14. Pars. 561 f.

15. *Memories, Dreams, Reflections*, pp. 36 ff. (pp. 47 ff.).

16. *Ibid.*, p. 222 (p. 211).

17. "Reply to Martin Buber", Coll. Works, Vol. 18 (in preparation).

18. "Answer to Job", par. 736.

19. *Ibid.*, par. 733. The passage reads in full: "A sea of grace is met by a seething lake of fire, and the light of love glows with a fierce dark heat of which it is said 'ardet non lucet'—it burns but gives no light. That is the eternal as distinct from the temporal gospel: *one can love God but must fear him.*"

20. *Jenseits von Schuld und Sühne.*   21. *Ibid.*, p. 29.   22. *Ibid.*, p. 31.

23. *Memories, Dreams, Reflections*, p. 359 (p. 330).

## 9. The Individuation of Mankind

1. *Psychology and Alchemy*, par. 556.

2. *Psychology and Religion*, par. 141. The modern assumption of an "original monotheism" is of no relevance in this context.

3. "Dogma of the Trinity", par. 206.

4. Cf. "The Psychology of the Transference", par. 396: "Have the Churches adapted themselves to this secular change? Their truth may, with more right than we realise, call itself 'eternal', but its temporal garment must pay tribute to the evanescence of all earthly things and should take account

of psychic changes. Eternal truth needs a human language that alters with the spirit of the times. The primordial images undergo ceaseless transformation and yet remain ever the same, but only in a new form can they be understood anew. Always they require a new interpretation . . ." For Goethe, God was "in the evolving and self-transforming, not in the evolved and torpid". Eckermann, *Conversations with Goethe*, entry for 13 February 1829.

5. Strictly speaking, by "the man of today" we mean those who at any period live in a spiritual "today". There are also at any period valid ways of life that belong to the past: even today there is the way of life of the mediaeval man, the eighteenth century rationalist, the nineteenth century romantic, etc.

6. "The Psychology of the Transference", par. 390. For a case history of the God-image as constellated in the unconscious of a modern man see particularly the first paper in *Psychology and Religion*.

7. The mathematician Andreas Speiser agrees with Jung: "Above all we must guard against believing that we have understood 'God' with the word 'Trinity'. It is, on the contrary, merely a question of what to our way of thinking is the most correct way to speak of God, or rather, to name him." "Platonische Lehre vom unbekannten Gott", *Eranos-Jahrbuch 1940/41*, p. 23.

8. It is not Jung's book that gives the answer to Job, though it is constantly, and quite incomprehensibly, misunderstood in this sense. Cf. par. 647: With Christ's "despairing cry from the Cross: 'My God, my God, why hast thou forsaken me?' . . . God experiences what it means to be a mortal man and drinks to the dregs what he made his faithful servant Job suffer." For the intermediate stages in the transformation of the God-image as documented by Ezekiel, Daniel and Enoch see pars. 662–87.

9. Par. 740.

10. Jung's use of the word "myth" for the Christian message implies no depreciation of its numinous reality but is rather what Thomas Mann calls the "garment of the mystery". According to Tillich, religion can express itself only in "the symbol and the united group of symbols which we call myths". From "The Meaning and Justification of Religious Symbols", in *Religious Experience and Truth* (a symposium edited by Sidney Hook), p. 3.

11. *Memories, Dreams, Reflections*, pp. 331 f. (p. 306).

12. "A Psychological Approach to the Dogma of the Trinity", par. 236. Cf. *Memories, Dreams, Reflections*, p. 333 (p. 307): "A further development of the myth might well begin with the outpouring of the Holy Spirit upon the apostles, by which they were made into sons of God, and not only they, but all others who through them and after them received the *filiatio*—the sonship of God."

13. "Answer to Job", pars. 693, 741, 746.
14. "Dogma of the Trinity", par. 238.    15. *Ibid.*, par. 289.
16. In *Aion* Jung shows that even in Christianity secret attempts were made to unite Christ and the devil or God and the devil. At the beginning of the second millennium numerous heretical sects were formed which included the devil in their teachings, often as the "dark brother of Christ". Also, the alchemical "spirit Mercurius" is a symbol of that dark power which was excluded from Christian dogma, though for the alchemists it remained connected with Christian ideas. In addition, there are well-known myths and folk tales in which the same power and eternality are ascribed to the devil as to God at the work of creation. In the Gnostic view, the devil, in the form of the demiurge, was the sole creator of the world.
17. "Answer to Job", par. 740.    18. *Ibid.*, par. 746.
19. *Ibid.*, par. 742.    20. "Dogma of the Trinity", par. 260.
21. *Der unbehauste Mensch*, p. 50. Equally daring paradoxes appear in alchemical descriptions of the spirit Mercurius, who is devil and psychopompic saviour at once. As *ignis mercurialis* (mercurial fire) he is also hell-fire, in which "God himself burns in divine love". ("Gloria mundi", *Musaeum Hermeticum*, p. 246.) Cf. "The Spirit Mercurius", in *Alchemical Studies*, par. 257, also *Psychology and Alchemy*, par. 446.
22. *Memories, Dreams, Reflections*, p. 338 (pp. 311 ff.).
23. Cf. "The Psychology of the Transference", par. 537, where Jung cites Nicholas of Cusa: "Beyond this coincidence of creating and being created art thou God."
24. The third bishop of Rome (92–102) after Peter.
25. "Answer to Job", p. 358.
26. *Memories, Dreams, Reflections*, p. 340 (p. 313).
27. "Dogma of the Trinity", par. 238.

### 10. Man in the Work of Redemption
1. Cf. Schärf, *Satan in the Old Testament*, and Hurwitz, *Die Gestalt des sterbenden Messias* (Studien aus dem C. G. Jung-Institut, VIII).
2. Cf. *Aion*, par. 105.
3. Scholem, *Major Trends in Jewish Mysticism*, especially the chapter "Isaac Luria and his School", pp. 244–86. Luria taught in Safed, Upper Galilee. Scholem calls him "a central figure of the later Kabbala".
4. *Ibid.*, p. 268. Cf. "Answer to Job", par. 595, n. 6.
5. *Major Trends*, p. 276.    6. *Ibid.*
7. *Ibid.*, p. 275.    8. *Ibid.*, p. 273.
9. *Memories, Dreams, Reflections*, p. 340 (p. 313).
10. "Dogma of the Trinity", par. 279.
11. *Ibid.*, par. 222.

12. Cf. *Psychology and Alchemy*, par. 17: "Psychology thus does just the opposite of what it is accused of: it provides possible approaches to a better understanding of these things, it opens people's eyes to the real meaning of dogmas and, far from destroying, it throws open an empty house to new inhabitants." See also "Dogma of the Trinity", par. 293.

13. *Psychology and Alchemy*, par. 329.

### *11. The One Reality*

1. Letter, October, 1954.          2. Cf. *Aion*, pars. 137 ff.

3. "Dogma of the Trinity", pars. 268 ff. Also Allenby, "Religionspsychologie—mit besonderer Berücksichtigung von C. G. Jung". *Psychotherapie und religiöse Erfahrung*.

4. Cf. "Transference", par. 392: "sectarian insistence is trying to corner him against his better judgment—tempting him to sin against the Holy Ghost".

5. Quoted in Heisenberg, "Wolfgang Paulis philosophische Auffassungen", in *Zeitschrift für Parapsychologie und Grenzgebiete der Psychologie*, III: 2/3, p. 127.

6. Quoted in Holthusen, *Der unbehauste Mensch*, p. 35.

7. "Dogma of the Trinity", par. 272.

8. "Answer to Job", pars. 658, 741, 749.

9. *Ibid.*, par. 748. For the difference between the psychological and theological interpretation of the dogma see section XIX.

10. "Answer to Job", par. 752.

11. According to the dogma, Mary was taken up to heaven with her body. Cf. "Dogma of the Trinity", par. 251.

12. Cf. Schubart, *Religion und Eros*. In Jung's psychology the interconnection of religion and Eros is directly due to the numinosity of the psychoid archetype.

13. Cf. "Transference", par. 392.

14. "Opposites are not contradictions but complements."

15. "The Influence of Archetypal Ideas on the Scientific Theories of Kepler", in *The Interpretation of Nature and the Psyche*, p. 208.

16. *Ibid.*

17. Cf. "On the Nature of the Psyche", par. 440.

18. *Mysterium Coniunctionis*, par. 768.

19. Cf. in particular Anrich, *Moderne Physik und Tiefenpsychologie*.

20. "Spirit and Life", in *The Structure and Dynamics of the Psyche*, par. 619.

### *12. The Individual*

1. "The Undiscovered Self", in *Civilization in Transition*, par. 511.

2. "Answer to Job", par. 734

3. "The Meaning of Psychology for Modern Man", in *Civilization in Transition*, par. 315. Cf. also "The Role of the Unconscious", *ibid.*, par. 45: "In reality only a change of attitude in the individual can bring about a renewal of the nations."

4. "Psychotherapy Today", in *The Practice of Psychotherapy*, par. 227.

5. *Ibid.*, par. 229. The passage reads in full: "And inasmuch as we are convinced that the individual is the carrier of life, we have served life's purpose if one tree at least succeeds in bearing fruit, though a thousand others remain barren. Anyone who proposed to bring all growing things to the highest pitch of development would soon find the weeds—those hardest of perennials—waving above his head. I therefore consider it the prime task of psychotherapy today to pursue with singleness of purpose the goal of individual development. So doing, our efforts will follow nature's own striving to bring life to the fullest possible fruition in each individual, for only in the individual can life fulfil its meaning—not in the bird that sits in a golden cage."

6. "The Undiscovered Self", par. 588.

7. Cf. Tillich, *The Protestant Era*.

8. *Ibid.*, p. 231.                    9. *Ibid.*, p. 233 (modified).

10. Cf. "Dogma of the Trinity", par. 292 end: "Civilisation does not consist in progress as such and in mindless destruction of old values, but in developing and refining the good that has been won."

### 13. Meaning as the Myth of Consciousness

1. Literally, a "bending back".

2. Cf. *Memories, Dreams, Reflections*, p. 338 (p. 312): "By virtue of his reflective faculties, man is raised out of the animal world, and by his mind he demonstrates that nature has put a high premium precisely upon the development of consciousness." Research into animal behaviour has shown that animals do not act only out of fixed instinctual drives but have the capacity to adapt to altered conditions of life. There is no difference in principle between men and animals, though there is a quantitative as well as qualitative difference of awareness.

3. *Ibid.*, pp. 338 f. (p. 312).

4. Cf. "Psychological Aspects of the Mother Archetype", in *The Archetypes and the Collective Unconscious*, par. 177.

5. *Memories, Dreams, Reflections*, pp. 255 f. (p. 240).

6. Cf. *supra*, l.c. pp. 124 f., and *infra*, p. 142.

7. *Memories, Dreams, Reflections*, p. 339 (p. 312).          8. *Ibid.*

9. Büttner, *Meister Eckeharts Schriften und Predigten*, I, p. 1.

10. "Lob der Vergänglichkeit", in *Altes und Neues*, p. 376. Cf. Julian Huxley, *Evolution in Action*, p. 132: "(Man) need no longer regard himself

as insignificant in the cosmos. He is intensely significant. In his person, he has acquired meaning, for he is constantly creating new meanings."

11. Jung was neither a Nazi sympathiser nor an antisemite, despite constant assertions to the contrary. This will become quite apparent from the publication of letters written during the thirties and forties. See *Civilization in Transition*, Appendix; also Jaffé, "C. G. Jung und National Socialism", in *From the Life and Work of C. G. Jung*.

12. Cf. "Psychological Aspects of the Mother Archetype", par. 177: " 'But why on earth,' you may ask, 'should it be necessary for man to achieve, by hook or by crook, a higher level of consciousness?' This is truly the critical question, and I do not find the answer easy. Instead of a real answer I can only make a confession of faith: I believe that, after thousands and millions of years, someone had to realise that this wonderful world of mountains and oceans, suns and moons, galaxies and nebulae, plants and animals, exists." Then follows the passage referred to in n. 4 above, ending: "Every advance, even the smallest, along this path of conscious realisation adds that much to the world."

13. *Memories, Dreams, Reflections*, p. 338 (p. 312).

14. *Ibid.*, p. 339 (pp. 312 f.).      15. *Ibid.*, p. 222 (p. 211).

16. Cf. *Memories, Dreams, Reflections*, p. 339 (p. 312): "If the Creator were conscious of himself, he would not need conscious creatures; nor is it probable that the extremely indirect methods of creation, which squander millions of years upon the development of countless species and creatures, are the outcome of purposeful intention."

17. Serrano, *C. G. Jung and Hermann Hesse*, p. 88.

18. For a comprehensive survey and interpretation see Corti, "Die Mythopoese des 'Werdenden Gottes'," *Archiv für genetische Philosophie* (Zürich 1953), and "Der Mensch als Organ Gottes", *Eranos-Jahrbuch 1959*.

19. Ch. V, 4 (b): "The Relativity of the Idea of God in Meister Eckhart".

20. *Ibid.*, Büttner, *Meister Eckeharts Schriften und Predigten*, I, p. 198.

21. Cited in Corti, "Der Mensch als Organ Gottes", pp. 403 f.

22. "Das Stundenbuch", Book I. In *Ausgewählte Werke*, I, p. 29.

23. "Answer to Job", par. 555.

24. *Memories, Dreams, Reflections*, p. 340 (p. 313). Cf. Einstein, *The World as I See It*, p. 1: "What is the meaning of human life, or of organic life altogether? To answer this question at all implies a religion. Is there any sense then, you may ask, in putting it? I answer, the man who regards his own life and that of his fellow creatures as meaningless is not only unfortunate but almost disqualified for life."

25. "Psychotherapists or the Clergy", in *Psychology and Religion*, par. 497.

26. *Memories, Dreams, Reflections*, p. 340 (p. 313).

27. *The Archetypes and the Collective Unconscious*, par. 64.

M

28. *The Trial* (Penguin Modern Classics), pp. 235 f.

29. *The Archetypes and the Collective Unconscious*, par. 66.

30. *Ibid.*, pars. 66, 79.

31. Cf. Jung, "Commentary on The Secret of the Golden Flower", in *Alchemical Studies*, par. 45: "(The images of the unconscious) cannot be thought up but must grow again from the forgotten depths if they are to express the supreme insights of consciousness and the loftiest intuitions of the spirit, and in this way fuse the uniqueness of present-day consciousness with the age-old past of life."

32. Letter, March 1933.

33. "Psychotherapists or the Clergy", par. 520; *Mysterium Coniunctionis*, par. 759.

34. Cf. "Synchronicity: An Acausal Connecting Principle", in *The Structure and Dynamics of the Psyche*, par. 843.

35. How frequent they are is not easy to determine. Perhaps they would appear more frequent if one were on the lookout for them.

36. "Synchronicity", par. 849.     37. *Ibid.*, par. 958.

38. Swedenborg's visionary perception of a great fire in Stockholm while he was in Göteborg, some fifty miles away, is a synchronistic phenomenon characterised by an objective simultaneity: the fire was actually raging in Stockholm at the same time. The case is reported and authenticated by Kant in his *Dreams of a Spirit-Seer, Illustrated by Dreams of Metaphysics*, pp. 155 ff. (See also "Synchronicity", par. 912.) Goethe's encounter with his future self as a Doppelgänger, after his farewell from Friederike Brion, is a genuine synchronistic phenomenon too, though here the simultaneity was experienced subjectively: the real event in the future became an inner experience here and now.

39. "Synchronicity", par. 948. Cf. *ibid.*, par. 942: "Synchronicity postulates a meaning which is *a priori* in relation to human consciousness and apparently outside man."

40. *Ibid.*, par. 965: "The meaningful coincidence or equivalence of a psychic and a physical state that have no causal relationship to one another means, in general terms, that it is a modality without a cause, an 'acausal orderedness'." Cf. par. 942, n. 71: "In view of the possibility that synchronicity is not only a psychophysical phenomenon but might also occur without the participation of the human psyche, I should like to point out that in this case we would have to speak not of *meaning* but of equivalence or conformity."

41. Cf. Muschg, *Goethes Glaube an das Dämonische*, p. 23. The above use of the term "daemonic" occurs in *Dichtung und Wahrheit*, Part IV, Book, 20.

42. "The Influence of Archetypal Ideas on the Scientific Theories of Kepler", in *The Interpretation of Nature and the Psyche*, p. 152.

# Bibliography

# Bibliography

ABELL, A. M. *Gespräche mit berühmten Komponisten.* Garmisch-Partenkirschen, 1962.

ADLER, Gerhard. *The Living Symbol.* Bollingen Series LXIII (Pantheon Books). New York, 1961.
"Die Sinnfrage in der Psychotherapie". In: *Psychotherapeutische Probleme.* Studien aus dem C. G. Jung-Institut, XVII. Zurich, 1964. (Translation: "On the Question of Meaning in Psychotherapy", *Spring,* 1963. Published by the Analytical Psychology Club of New York.)

ALLENBY, A. I. "Religionspsychologie—mit besonderer Berücksichtigung von C. G. Jung". In: *Psychotherapie und religiöse Erfahrung.* Edited by W. Bitter, Stuttgart, 1965.

ALVERDES, F. "Die Wirksamkeit von Archetypen in den Instinkthandlungen der Tiere". In: *Zoologischer Anzeiger,* Bd. 119, Heft 9/10. Leipzig, 1937.

AMERY, J. *Jenseits von Schuld und Sühne.* Bewältigungsversuche eines Ueberwältigten. Munich, 1966.

ANGELUS SILESIUS (Johannes Scheffler). "Der Cherubinische Wandersmann". In: *Sämtliche Poetische Werke,* III. Edited by Hans Ludwig Held. 3 vols. Munich, 1949-52.

ANRICH, E. *Moderne Physik und Tiefenpsychologie.* Stuttgart, 1963.

AUGUSTINE, SAINT. *Liber de Spiritu et Anima.* In: MIGNE, Jacques Paul (ed.). *Patrologiae cursus completus.* P.L., Vol. 40, cols. 779-832.

BARNETT, L. K. *The Universe and Dr. Einstein.* London, 1950.

BAVINK, B. *Die Naturwissenschaft auf dem Wege zur Religion.* Basel, 1948.

BITTER, W. (ed.). *Psychotherapie und religiöse Erfahrung.* Stuttgart, 1965.

BOEHME, Jacob. *Werke.* Edited by K. W. Schiebler. 7 vols. Leipzig, 1831-47.

CORTI, W. R. "Der Mensch als Organ Gottes". In: *Eranos-Jahrbuch 1959.* Zürich, 1960.

—— "Die Mythopoese des 'werdenden Gottes' ". In: *Archiv für genetische Philosophie.* Zürich, 1953.

ECKEHART, MEISTER. *Schriften und Predigten*. Edited by H. Büttner. 3 vols. Jena, 1917. (Translation: C. de B. Evans, *Meister Eckhart*. 2 vols. London, 1924–52.)

EINSTEIN, Albert. *The World as I See It*. Translated by Alan Harris. The Thinker's Library, No. 79. London, 1940.

ELIADE, Mircea. "La Coincidentia Oppositorum et la mystère de la totalité". In: *Eranos-Jahrbuch 1959*. Zürich, 1960.

—— *Schmiede und Alchemisten*. Stuttgart, 1966.

ELIOT, T. S. *Four Quartets*. London, 1959.

FIERZ, H. K. "Sinn im Wahn". In: *Klinik und analytische Psychologie*. Studien aus dem C. G. Jung-Institut, XV. Zürich, 1963.

FREY-ROHN, L. "Evil from the Psychological Point of View". In: *Evil*. Studies in Jungian Thought. Translated by Ralph Manheim and Hildegard Nagel. Evanston (Illinois), 1967.

GOETHE, Johann Wolfgang von. *Dichtung und Wahrheit*. Leipzig, 1917.

—— *Eckermann's Conversations with Goethe*. Translated by R. O. Moon. London, 1951.

—— *Goethes Gespräche ohne die Gespräche mit Eckermann*. Edited by F. Freiherr von Biedermann. Leipzig, n.d.

HAFTMANN, W. *Paul Klee, Wege bildnerischen Denkens*. Munich, 1955.

HAMMARSKJÖLD, Dag. *Markings*. Translated by Leif Sjöberg and W. H. Auden. London, 1964.

—— *Happenings*. Edited by J. Becker and W. Vostell. Hamburg, 1965.

HARDING, Esther. *Woman's Mysteries*. Foreword by C. G. Jung. New York, 1955.

HEISENBERG, W. *The Physicist's Conception of Nature*. Translated by Arnold J. Pomerans. London, 1958.

—— "Wolfgang Paulis philosophische Auffassungen". In: *Zeitschrift für Parapsychologie und Grenzgebiete der Psychologie*, Bd. III, Nr. 2/3. Bern, 1960.

HEITLER, W. *Der Mensch und die naturwissenschaftliche Erkenntnis*. 3rd edn. Braunschweig, 1964.

HESS, W. *Dokumente zum Verständnis der modernen Malerei*. Hamburg, 1958.

HOLTHUSEN, H. E. *Der unbehauste Mensch*. Munich, 1964.

HUCH, Richarda. *Der Sinn der Heiligen Schrift*. Leipzig, 1919.

HURWITZ, S. *Die Gestalt des sterbenden Messias*. Studien aus dem C. G. Jung-Institut, VIII. Zürich, 1958.

HUXLEY, Aldous. *The Doors of Perception*. London, 1954.

—— *Heaven and Hell*. London, 1956.

HUXLEY, Julian. *Evolution in Action*. London, 1953.

JACOBI, Jolande. *Complex/Archetype/Symbol in the Psychology of C. G. Jung*. Translated by Ralph Manheim. New York and London, 1959.

JACOBI, Jolande *The Way of Individuation*. Translated by R. F. C. Hull. London and New York, 1967.

JAFFÉ, Aniela. "C. G. Jung and National Socialism". In: *From the Life and Work of C. G. Jung*. Translated by R. F. C. Hull. New York, 1970; London, 1971.

—— "Symbolism in the Visual Arts". In: *Man and his Symbols*. Edited by C. G. Jung. London, 1964.

JORDAN, Pascual. *Der Naturwissenschaftler von der religiösen Frage*. Oldenburg, 1963.

JUNG, Carl Gustav. "The Aims of Psychotherapy". In: *The Practice of Psychotherapy*, q.v.

—— *Aion*. Collected Works, 9 Part II. London and New York, 1959. (2nd printing with corrections, 1968.)

—— *Alchemical Studies*. Collected Works, 13. London and New York, 1967.

—— "Analytical Psychology and *Weltanschauung*". In: *The Structure and Dynamics of the Psyche*, q.v.

—— "Answer to Job". In: *Psychology and Religion: West and East*, q.v.

—— *The Archetypes and the Collective Unconscious*. Collected Works, 9 Part I. London and New York, 1959. (2nd printing with corrections, 1970.)

—— "Brother Klaus". In: *Psychology and Religion*, q.v.

—— *Civilization in Transition*. Collected Works, 10. London and New York, 1964.

—— "Commentary on *The Secret of the Golden Flower*". In: *Alchemical Studies*, q.v.

—— "Concerning the Archetypes, with Special Reference to the Anima Concept". In: *The Archetypes and the Collective Unconscious*.

—— "Concerning Rebirth". In: *ibid*.

—— *The Development of Personality*. Collected Works, 17. London and New York (2nd printing), 1964.

—— "Foreword to Harding's *Woman's Mysteries*". In: Collected Works, 18 (in preparation).

—— "Foreword to Suzuki's *Introduction to Zen Buddhism*". In: *Psychology and Religion*, q.v.

—— "Freud and Jung: Contrasts". In: *Freud and Psychoanalysis*, q.v.

—— *Freud and Psychoanalysis*. Collected Works, 4. London and New York, 1961.

—— "Good and Evil in Analytical Psychology". In: *Civilization in Transition*, q.v.

—— "The Holy Men of India". In: *Psychology and Religion*, q.v.

—— "Instinct and the Unconscious". In: *The Structure and Dynamics of the Psyche*, q.v.

JUNG, Carl Gustav. "The Meaning of Psychology for Modern Man". In *Civilization in Transition*, q.v.

—— "Medicine and Psychotherapy". In: *The Practice of Psychotherapy*, q.v.

—— *Memories, Dreams, Reflections*. Recorded and Edited by Aniela Jaffé. Translated by Richard and Clara Winston. London and New York, 1963. (The two editions have different pagination.)

—— *Mysterium Coniunctionis*. Collected Works, 14. London and New York, 1967. (2nd printing with corrections, 1970.)

—— "On the Nature of the Psyche". In: *The Structure and Dynamics of the Psyche*, q.v.

—— "On Psychic Energy". In: *ibid.*

—— *The Practice of Psychotherapy*. Collected Works, 16. London and New York (2nd edition, revised and augmented), 1966.

—— *The Psychogenesis of Mental Disease*. Collected Works, 3. London and New York, 1960.

—— "A Psychological Approach to the Dogma of the Trinity". In: *Psychology and Religion*, q.v.

—— "Psychological Aspects of the Mother Archetype". In: *The Archetypes and the Collective Unconscious*, q.v.

—— "Psychological Commentary on *The Tibetan Book of the Dead*". In: *Psychology and Religion*, q.v.

—— "Psychological Commentary on *The Tibetan Book of the Great Liberation*". In: *ibid.*

—— *Psychological Types*. Collected Works, 6 (in preparation). Alternate source: Translation by H. G. Baynes. London and New York, 1923.

—— "A Psychological View of Conscience". In: *Civilisation in Transition*, q.v.

—— *Psychology and Alchemy*. Collected Works, 12. London and New York (2nd edition, completly revised), 1968.

—— "The Psychology of the Child Archetype". In: *The Archetypes and the Collective Unconscious*, q.v.

—— *Psychology and Religion: West and East*. Collected Works, 11. London and New York (2nd printing with corrections), 1963. (3rd printing with further corrections, 1970.)

—— "The Psychology of the Transference". In: *The Practice of Psychotherapy*, q.v.

—— "Psychotherapists or the Clergy". In: *Psychology and Religion*, q.v.

—— "Psychotherapy and a Philosophy of Life". In: *The Practice of Psychotherapy*, q.v.

—— "Psychotherapy Today". In: *ibid.*

—— "Reply to Martin Buber". In: Collected Works, 18 (in preparation). Alternate source: Jung, *Gesammelte Werke*, XI. *Zur Psychologie westlicher und östlicher Religion*. Zürich, 1963.

JUNG, Carl Gustav. "The Role of the Unconscious". In: *Civilization in Transition*, q.v.

—— "Schizophrenia". In: The *Psychogenesis of Mental Disease*, q.v.

—— "Spirit and Life". In: *The Structure and Dynamics of the Psyche*, q.v.

—— "The Spirit Mercurius". In: *Alchemical Studies*, q.v.

—— "The Stages of Life". In: *The Structure and Dynamics of the Psyche*, q.v.

—— *The Structure and Dynamics of the Psyche*. Collected Works, 8. London and New York, 1960. (2nd printing with corrections, 1970.)

—— "The Structure of the Psyche". In: *ibid*.

—— "A Study in the Process of Individuation". In: *The Archetypes and the Collective Unconscious*, q.v.

—— *Symbols of Transformation*. Collected Works, 5. London and New York (2nd edition with corrections), 1967.

—— "Synchronicity: An Acausal Connecting Principle". In: *The Structure and Dynamics of the Psyche*, q.v.

—— "Transformation Symbolism in the Mass". In: *Psychology and Religion*, q.v.

—— "The Transcendent Function". In: *The Structure and Dynamics of the Psyche*, q.v.

—— *Two Essays on Analytical Psychology*. Collected Works, 7. London and New York (revised edition), 1966.

—— "The Undiscovered Self". In: *Civilization in Transition*, q.v.

KAFKA, Franz. *The Trial*. Translated by Willa and Edwin Muir. Penguin Modern Classics. London, 1953.

KANDINSKY, W. *Ueber das Geistige in der Kunst*. 6th edn. Bern-Bümpliz, 1959.

KANT, Immanuel. *The Critique of Pure Reason*. Translated by J. M. D. Meiklejohn. Everyman's Library. London and New York, 1934.

—— *Dreams of a Spirit-Seer, Illustrated by Dreams of Metaphysics*. Translated by E. F. Goerwitz. London, 1900.

KAZANTZAKIS, N. *Report to Greco*. Translated by P. A. Bien. Oxford, 1965.

KERÉNYI, Karl. "Mescalin-Perioden der Religionsgeschichte". In: *Wege zum Menschen*, 17. Jhg., Heft 6, 1965.

—— *Umgang mit Göttlichem*. Göttingen, 1961.

—— "Voraussetzung der Einweihung in Eleusis". In: *Initiation*. Edited by C. J. Bleeker. Leiden, 1965.

LAING, R. D. *The Politics of Experience and the Bird of Paradise*. Penguin Original. London, 1967. Different printing, New York (Pantheon), 1967.

LILJE, H. *Martin Luther in Selbstzeugnissen und Bilddokumenten*. Hamburg, 1965.

MANN, Thomas. Letter to Ida Herz, 21.3.1954. In: *Neue Rundschau*, Heft 2. Zürich, 1965.

MANN, Thomas. "Lob der Vergänglichkeit". In: *Altes und Neues*. Kleine Prosa aus fünf Jahrzehnten. Frankfurt am Main, 1953.

MASTERS, R. E. L. and HOUSTON, Jean. *The Varieties of Psychedelic Experience*. New York, 1966.

—— *Musaeum Hermeticum*. Frankfurt am Main, 1678.

MUSCHG, W. *Goethes Glaube an das Dämonische*. Stuttgart, 1958.

NEUMANN, Erich. "Dank an Jung". In: *Der Psychologe*, VII. Schwarzenburg, 1955.

—— *Depth Psychology and a New Ethic*. With a foreword by C. G. Jung. Translated by Eugene Rolfe. London, 1969.

—— "Die Sinnfrage und das Individuum". In: *Eranos-Jahrbuch 1957*. Zürich, 1958.

NEWLAND, Constance A. *My Self and I*. New York, 1962.

NOWACKI, W. *Die Idee einer Struktur der Wirklichkeit*. Mitteilungen der Naturforschenden Gesellschaft. Neue Folge, Bd. 14. Bern, 1954.

OPPENHEIMER, J. Robert. *Science and the Common Understanding*. BBC Reith Lectures, 1953. Oxford University Press, 1954.

OTTO, R. *The Idea of the Holy*. Translated by J. W. Harvey. Oxford, 1926; New York, 1950; London (Pelican Books), 1959.

PAULI, Wolfgang. "The Influence of Archetypal Ideas on the Scientific Theories of Kepler". Translated by Priscilla Silz. In: *The Interpretation of Nature and the Psyche*. London and New York, 1955.

—— "Naturwissenschaftliche und erkenntnistheoretische Aspekte der Ideen vom Unbewussten". In: *Dialectica*, Bd. 8, Nr. 4. Neûchatel, 1954.

PORTMANN, A. *Biologie und Geist*. Zürich, 1956.

—— "Freiheit und Bindung in biologischer Sicht". In: *Eranos-Jahrbuch 1962*. Zürich, 1963.

—— "Gestaltung als Lebensvorgang". In: *Eranos-Jahrbuch 1960*. Zürich, 1961.

—— "Das Lebendige als vorbereitete Beziehung". In: *Eranos-Jahrbuch 1955*. Zürich, 1956.

—— "Sinnbedeutung als biologisches Problem". In: *Eranos-Jahrbuch 1957*. Zürich, 1958.

READ, Herbert. *A Concise History of Modern Painting*. London, 1959.

RILKE, Rainer Maria. "Das Stundenbuch". In: *Ausgewählte Werke*, I. Edited by Ernst Zinn. 3rd edition. Reutlingen, 1948.

RUDIN, J. "C. G. Jung und die Religion". In *Orientierung*, 28 Jhg. (Nov. 15). Zürich, 1964.

—— *Psychotherapie und Religion*. Olten, 1964.

SALIS, J. R. von. "Geschichte als Prozess". In: *Transparente Welte*. Festschrift zum 60. Geburtstag von J. Gebser. Bern, 1965.

SARTRE, Jean-Paul. *The Flies*. Translated by Stuart Gilbert. London, 1946.
—— *Words*. Translated by Irene Clephane. London, 1964.
SCHÄR, H. "A Protestant View of Conscience". In: *Conscience*. Studies in Jungian Thought. Translated by R. F. C. Hull and Ruth Horine. Evanston (Illinois), 1970.
SCHÄRF, R. *Satan in the Old Testament*. Translated by Hildegard Nagel. Evanston (Illinois), 1967.
SCHOLEM, Gershom. "Gut und Böse in der Kabbala". In: *Eranos-Jahrbuch 1961*. Zürich, 1962.
—— *Major Trends in Jewish Mysticism*. Revised edition. New York, 1946.
—— "Die mystische Gestalt der Gottheit in der Kabbala". In: *Eranos-Jahrbuch 1960*. Zürich, 1961.
SCHUBART, W. *Religion und Eros*. Munich, 1966.
SERRANO, Miguel de. *C. G. Jung and Hermann Hesse*. London, 1966.
SILBERER, Herbert. *Problems of Mysticism and Its Symbolism*. Translated by Smith Ely Jelliffe. New York, 1917.
SPEISER, Andreas. "Die Platonische Lehre vom unbekannten Gott und die christliche Trinität". In: *Eranos-Jahrbuch 1940/41*. Zürich, 1942.
*The Ten Principal Upanishads*. Translated by Shree Purohit Swami and W. B. Yeats. London and New York, 1937.
*The Thirteen Principal Upanishads*. Translated by R. E. Hume. Oxford, 1934.
TILLICH, Paul. *Auf der Grenze*. Munich, 1962.
—— *The Courage to Be*. Fontana Library of Theology and Philosophy. London, 1962.
—— "The Meaning and Justification of Religious Symbols". In: *Religious Experience and Truth*. A symposium edited by Sidney Hook. Edinburgh, 1962.
—— "Das neue Sein als Zentralbegriff". In: *Eranos-Jahrbuch 1954*. Zürich, 1955.
—— *Die neue Wirklichkeit*. Munich, 1962.
—— *The Protestant Era*. Translated by James Luther Adams. London, 1951.
—— *Religionsphilosophie*. Stuttgart, 1962.
WATTS, A. W. *The Two Hands of God*. New York, 1963.
WEIBEL, E. R. "Modell und Wirklichkeit in der biologischen Forschung". In: *Neue Zürcher Zeitung*, Nr. 3809, 13 September 1964.
WEISS, V. *Die Gnosis J. Böhmes*. Zürich, 1955.
WEIZÄCKER, C. F. von. *The History of Nature*. Translated by Fred D. Wieck. London, 1951.
—— "Das Verhältnis der Quantenmechanik zur Philosophie Kants". In: *Zum Weltbild der Physik*. 7. Aufl. Stuttgart, 1958.
WERBLOWSKY, Zwi. "The Concept of Conscience in Jewish Perspective".

In: *Conscience*. Studies in Jungian Thought. Translated by R. F. C. Hull and Ruth Horine. Evanston (Illinois), 1970.

WEYL, H. "Wissenschaft als symbolische Konstruktion". In: *Eranos-Jahrbuch 1948*. Zürich, 1949.

WHYTE, L. *The Unconscious before Freud*. Anchor Books. New York, 1962.

WORRINGER, W. *Abstraction and Empathy*. (Orig. 1907.) Translated by Michael Bullock. London, 1953.

—— *Formprobleme der Gotik*. Munich, 1912.

ZIMMER, E. *Umsturz im Weltbild der Physik*. Munich, 1961.

**DAIMON**
ZÜRICH

---

*Daimon* (pronounced dī'mōn) originates from Socrates, who gave this name to the 'driving inner force' which accompanied and inspired him throughout his life.

More recently, the word *daimon* was adopted by the Swiss psychologist C.G.Jung (1875—1961) to designate a unique suprapersonal spirit inherent in everyone. It is understood to be free of value judgements and thus neither 'good' nor 'evil'; it simply *is*. Through our encounters with this inexplicable force, we live and grow as individuals.

In presenting the writings of some of today's leading European analysts, **Daimon Zürich** hopes to be making a contribution to this spirit. Our authors include, among others, the well-known writers and psychologists: Marie-Louise von Franz, Aniela Jaffé, Liliane Frey-Rohn, Siegmund Hurwitz, C.A.Meier, Toni Wolff and Erich Neumann.

For further information about **Daimon Zürich** titles, including our complete program in the original German, write to:

Daimon Verlag
Postfach
CH-**8024** Zürich
Switzerland